Priests
Identity and Ministry

Priests
Identity and Ministry

Edited by

Robert J. Wister

Michael Glazier, Inc.
Wilmington, Delaware

The Editor

Rev. Robert J. Wister is executive director of the seminary dept. of the National Catholic Education Association. He holds a doctorate in Ecclesiastic History from the Gregorian University in Rome. He is also assistant professor of Historical Studies in the School of Theology of Seton Hall University in South Orange, NJ.

First published in 1990 by Michael Glazier, Inc., 1935 West Fourth Street, Wilmington, Delaware 19805.

Library of Congress Cataloging-in-Publication Data

Priesthood: identity and ministry/editor. Robert Wister.

    p.   cm.

  ISBN: 0-89453-784-9

  1. Priesthood. 2. Catholic Church—Clergy. I. Wister, Robert James.

BX1912.P754 1989

262'.142—dc20   89-37106

                                  CIP

Cover Design by Pat Harris
Printed in the United States of America

Table of Contents

Preface

In his talk prepared for delivery at the Pontifical College Josephinum, Cardinal Baum stated that the Holy See's concern over the issue of "priestly identity" was the major motivation underlying the Apostolic Visitation of United States seminaries. The articles in this book were all prepared with that issue in mind. In each article, the author has addressed his or her topic with this theme underlying the presentation. It is their hope that they will be studied with this question uppermost in the mind of the reader.

The professional quality of this collection makes it a useful sourcebook for those preparing and taking courses in sacramental theology, especially those courses which focus on Holy Orders. The pastoral style of the articles makes them equally useful as a background for theological and spiritual reflection on the mystery of the priesthood.

Rev. Robert J. Wister
Executive Director
Seminary Department

Introduction

The theology of the priesthood has been a topic which has engendered a great deal of discussion in the period following the Second Vatican Council. Nowhere has it been as crucial as within the seminary community. When the Second Assembly of Rectors and Ordinaries met in 1986 at Seton Hall University, its focus was inexorably drawn to this issue. As the assembly drew to a close, it asked that further research be done to bring to the seminary community resources which would assist in the presentation of the theology of ordained priesthood within the seminary community.

The Executive Committee of the Seminary Department of the National Catholic Educational Association convened a group of scholars to reflect on the theology of ordained priesthood from the perspective of their expertise and specialization. The study group consisted of Donald Senior on the biblical testimony, Agnes Cunningham on the patristic evidence, John O'Malley on historical development, Peter Fink from the point of sacramental theology and Robert Schwartz on the contribution of the Second Vatican Council. Their reflections which developed into the papers presented here were the basis of a dialogue with the members of the Bishops Committee on Priestly Formation of the National Conference of Catholic Bishops.

This book represents the fruit of almost a year of reflection and dialogue. To the scholars' papers, we have added a paper by Bishop Buechlein, a member of the Bishops Committee on Priestly Formation, and the pastoral letter on priesthood of Archbishop Stafford. As an appendix, we have included remarks prepared by Cardinal Baum on the centrality of the issue of priestly identity in the recently completed Apostolic Visitation of American seminaries.

It is our hope that this publication will be useful to various communities and individuals. It will serve to assist the Bishops Committee on Formation as it directs the process to revise the *Program of Priestly Formation;* it will assist the seminary community and the wider theological community as it focuses on the theology of the priesthood; and it will, hopefully, stimulate discussion on this issue.

I would like to thank the Lilly Endowment and, in particular, Mr. Fred Hofheinz, for their continued interest in the quality of seminary and theological education. Funding from the endowment made possible the production and publication of these papers.

Biblical Foundations
for the Theology of Priesthood
Donald Senior, C.P.

The purpose of this study is to present some of the New Testament foundations for the theology of ordained priesthood. Much of it deals with historical questions concerning the evolution of ministry within the New Testament communities. This is necessary because the role of the presbyter or priest as it emerges in the patristic and later ages of the Church does not stand out clearly defined in the New Testament period. Attention to the historic origins of the order of priesthood is useful in constructing contemporary theology. The role of the presbyter or priest is in evolution today, as it was in the earliest periods of the Church's history. And many of the concerns about a theology of priesthood today derive from issues of structure and identity as much as they do from pure theological principles.

In laying out the biblical materials on these questions, I realize full well that the construction of a solid theology of priesthood will also need to consider post-biblical history, theological tradition, and other Church teaching. Therefore the biblical material cannot be the sole ingredient for a contemporary theology of priesthood.[1]

---

[1] A well balanced presentation of the New Testament materials and their implications for priesthood can be found in R. Brown, *Priest and Bishop: Biblical Reflections* (Paulist Press, 1970), and two more recent studies that build on this earlier work: *The Critical Meaning of the Bible* (Paulist Press, 1981), esp. pp. 96-106, 124-46; and *The Churches The Apostles Left Behind* (Paulist Press, 1984). Other works would include: B. Cooke, *Ministry to Word and Sacrament* (Fortress Press, 1976); E. Schillebeeckx, who emphasizes the evolution of Church order in *Ministry: Leadership in the*

Trying to do justice to the biblical data on this topic is a challenging task. My procedure will be to a) Discuss some issues of terminology and to enumerate some basic assumptions necessary for approaching the biblical materials; b) Consider the evolution and nature of pastoral leadership in the New Testament period and c) Draw some conclusions for a theology of priesthood today.

The Term "Priest" and the Biblical Materials

Some consideration of terminology is important at the outset. The term "priest" or "priesthood" is used in three different ways in Christian tradition: 1) The priesthood of Jesus Christ; 2) the priesthood of the faithful or the baptized; 3) the ordained ministry of priest.[2]

The New Testament uses the term "priest" only in connection with the first two senses. Jesus Christ is the priest or "highpriest" par excellence. As we will discuss later, Jesus' redemptive ministry of service, culminating in his death and resurrection, is the definitive act of priesthood, offering authentic obedient worship to God and atoning for the sins of humanity. Through Baptism, the Christian participates in this redemptive act of Christ and, as a community of faith and service, the Christians are a "priestly people" offering acceptable sacrifice to God.

For reasons we will discuss below, the New Testament does not apply the term "priest" to any office or specific function within the Christian community. That terminology appears in

Community of Jesus Christ (Crossroad, 1981) and his more recent expansion on this earlier study, *The Church with a Human Face* (Crossroad, 1985); N. Mitchell, *Mission and Ministry: History and Theology in the Sacrament of Order* (Message of the Sacraments 6; Michael Glazier, 1982). A study that reacts to some of the trends in contemporary Catholic scholarship is that of J. Galot, *Theology of the Priesthood* (San Francisco: Ignatius Press, 1985). An excellent survey of other pertinent literature is found in A. Lemaire, "The Ministries in the New Testament," *Biblical Theology Bulletin* 3 (1973), 133-169.

[2]On the interrelation of these notions of priesthood, see the very helpful essay of R. Brown, "Rethinking the Priesthood Biblically for All" in *Critical Meaning of the Bible*, pp. 96-106.

this sense only in the post-New Testament period. However, as this paper will attempt to illustrate, that does not mean that there are no points of continuity between the New Testament and the ordained ministry of presbyter or priest.

The office or function offering the closest analogy to the later designated office of "priest" is that of the episkopos/ presbyter. Whether the office of presbyter or bishop included a cultic or priestly function during the New Testament period cannot be fully determined. Since the term "presbyter" is biblically based and offers the broader scope for the functions of pastoral leadership and cultic leadership involved in contemporary ordained ministry, this paper will refer throughout to the term "presbyter."

Some Working Suppositions
in Considering the New Testament Evidence

Before turning specifically to the ministry of presbyter, I would like to cite some important basic assumptions in considering the New Testament data.

1) *The nature and form of ordained ministry, as with other aspects of the Church's life, are subject to ongoing development.* The Spirit which animated the first Christian communities, inspired the Scriptures, and sustained the mission of the Church, has remained present and active in the Church throughout the centuries. Therefore, developments in Church structures from New Testament times to the present are not necessarily an aberration but can be a sign of vitality. This is a basic conviction of Roman Catholic theology and is an important vantage point for approaching the biblical materials.

The New Testament evidence for various ministerial roles in the early Church, therefore, is important but not completely decisive for validating a particular ministry in the Church. A dialectic should exist between the scriptural witness and the ongoing life of the Church. Because Scripture as the Word of God expresses the very nature of the Church and is therefore normative for the Church's life, no ministry that lacks continuity and compatibility with the Scriptures can be legitimate. Because the Word of God also exists in the Church as a living tradition, evolution and development of the Church's structures are to be expected and are desirable and legitimate.

2) *All ministry, ordained and nonordained, has its basis in the redemptive mission of Jesus Christ.* Jesus of Nazareth inaugurated the Reign of God, bringing new life and hope to Israel, calling his community of disciples to conversion of heart and a share in his own mission. His obedient and life-giving ministry of teaching and healing met its supreme manifestation in his death and resurrection. The Risen Lord's continuing and living presence in the Church is the source and model for all genuine Christian ministry.

The Church in seeking to incarnate the Gospel of Jesus Christ draws its structures and instrumentalities, including its forms of ministry, not out of thin air but from models and patterns influenced by its surrounding cultural, political and social milieu.

3) Although the concern of this paper is a theology of "priesthood," as noted above *the term "priest" (hiereus) is never used in the New Testament to describe a particular Christian ministry.* The reasons for this absence are variously explained. Some scholars believe it was the result of a deliberate move away from the hierarchical structures of Judaism and a concurrent recognition of the inadequacy of the Old Testament cult. Others, by contrast, suggest that earliest Christianity did not question the validity of the Jewish priesthood and, there-fore, never contemplated—much less rejected—the idea of a Christian priesthood. This might be particularly true for the Jerusalem Church and for Jewish Christianity which kept close ties to Temple and its cult (see, for example, the opening chapters of Acts).

In the Epistle to the Hebrews Jesus' own priesthood is discussed but it is considered essentially different from that of the Old Testament cult and is by its nature unique and non-transferable. Jesus the Highpriest inaugurated the new and definitively efficacious sacrifice that eclipsed the ancient cult. Jesus exercised his priesthood not only through his sacrificial death and exaltation before God, but also through his com-passion and gracious service that united him with humanity.

While offering important insight in the redemptive work of

Christ and serving as a model of service and compassion for all Christian ministry, the priesthood described in Hebrews has no direct bearing on the role of the presbyter in the New Testament period and cannot be used to establish the existence of a priestly order in the New Testament Church.

4) Any continuity between the New Testament data and the role of ordained priest, therefore, cannot be on the level of terminology alone. An overall assessment of the New Testament data and subsequent historical developments suggests that *continuity is to be found on the level of certain functions* (e.g., community responsibility, pastoral care, leadership of cult, ministry of word, etc.) which in the earliest decades of the Church's existence were performed by various individuals and roles but which later (possibly by the end of the first, certainly in the second and third centuries) were combined into what will be called the office of the presbyter/episkopos.

5) The overall picture also suggests that whereas earliest Christianity did not use Jewish cultic terminology to describe leadership roles in the community (i.e., "priest," "highpriest"), *late second and third century Christianity returned to certain Old Testament models and terminology to describe cultic leadership in the community.* This may have been due to the fact that an understanding of the Eucharist as sacrifice was also becoming stronger at this period, thus providing a theological basis for applying "priestly" terminology to the leader of the Eucharist.

6) It should be noted that the *data available for making any statement about the precise nature, terminology, interrelationship and development of ministerial roles in the New Testament churches is sparse and difficult to interpret.* There are no New Testament texts which provide detailed information on the *functions* of various ministers. The lists in the Pastoral Epistles, for example, generally describe *qualifications* for office, not the functions of the office.[3] In addition, these lists are stereo-

---

[3]Cf., for example, I Timothy 3:1-3; Titus 1:5-9.

typed literary forms adapted from secular culture rather than unique creations of the Christian community.[4]

Because of the nature of the evidence, therefore, any statement about the historical evolution of ordained ministries in the New Testament period must be qualified. None of the New Testament books sets out to describe in detail the organizational chart of the Early Church. The information we do have comes as *obiter dicta* and is necessarily incomplete (as some commentators have pointed out, we have evidence that the Eucharist was celebrated in the Pauline churches only because Paul addressed some of the abuses taking place in the Corinthian Church!).

What is certain, however, is that in the second century and more obviously in the third the tradition of an ordained hierarchical ministry (i.e., bishop surrounded by priests, with authority in the community and leadership of cult) is firmly in place. How much of this was in place in the New Testament period and how uniform such structures may have been in the various New Testament churches are impossible to determine on the basis of the New Testament texts themselves.

7) *The New Testament data suggests considerable diversity existed in the early Church in its ministerial structures as in other areas of its life.* This diversity is both synchronic and diachronic. "Synchronic" in that different patterns existed in different churches at the same time: e.g., the governance of the Jerusalem Church may have been much more hierarchically structured, with the "Twelve" having a general policy and supervisory role and the local Church itself under the leadership of James and other elders. Some of the Pauline Churches, by contrast, may have been less structured at this period. "Diachronic" in that by the last quarter of the New Testament period there is clear evidence of a move toward a more formal and standard hierarchical mode of Church governance than in the earlier, more informal and charismatic structures existing in the first four or five decades of the Church's history.

---

[4]The virtues demanded of the episkopos are very similar, for example, to those required of the general in Osonander's *De imperatoris officio;* see M. Dibelius/ H. Conzelmann, *The Pastoral Epistles* (Hermeneia Commentaries: Philadelphia: Fortress, 1972), 158-159.

A New Testament Basis
for the Ordained Ministry of Priest

While the New Testament evidence points to some diversity of expression and some evolution in Church order, one can still trace continuity between the New Testament data and the ordained ministry of presbyter or priest that emerges more clearly in the post-biblical period.

The following points should be noted:

1) *The redemptive mission of Jesus is the ultimate basis for priestly ministry in the church.*

Jesus was not a member of the Levitical priesthood. However, the New Testament affirms that Jesus' life and ministry had cultic or sacrificial significance, that is, a meaning and intent associated with the meaning and intent of the Jewish cult. For example, there is an emphasis on the dedication of Jesus to his Father's will (cf. Lk 2:49; Mt 3:15; Jn 17:9 etc.), a motif that seems to draw on the cultic theme of dedication;[5] and his death, as the supreme manifestation of his mission, is interpreted in sacrifical terminology as a death "for the many" (Mk 10:45; 14:24), "for sins" (Mt 26:28; cf. 1:21). Jesus' death is, therefore, the fullest expression of a life of service for the other.

Hebrews describes the entire death-exaltation spectrum of Jesus' mission through an extended comparison with the Jewish priesthood, temple and liturgy. Here, too, Jesus' compassion and service to others are singled out as characteristic of his priestly ministry. Paul, I Peter and other New Testament traditions describe Jesus' death as "atonement" for sin. By extension, the Risen Christ is considered the new "temple" (cf. Mk 12:10-11; 14:48; Mt 21:42; Jn 2:18-22).

Thus there is broad New Testament support for the use of cultic categories and language to describe the full span of Jesus' redemptive mission.

Through baptism the Christian participates in the death-

---

[5] Cf., on this point, B. Cooke, *Ministry to Word and Sacrament,* p. 526.

resurrection of Jesus and becomes a member of Christ's body. The Christian is, in Paul's terminology, "in Christ," participating in Christ's mission. Therefore, certain New Testament traditions ascribe a cultic character and cultic action to the Christian community as a whole. In its own dedication to God's will, its holiness and life of service made possible through faith in Christ, the Church itself is a "priestly people," offering "spiritual worship" to God (cf. I Peter 2:4, 9; I Cor 10:31; Rom 12:1).

Recent Catholic official teaching on the nature of ordained priesthood, therefore, properly uses the priesthood of the community—which in turn is based on the priesthood of Jesus— as the basic starting point for speaking of a New Testament basis for the ordained "priesthood."[6]

From its earliest moments, the Christian community performed ritual acts which were understood to have cultic significance, namely Baptism and Eucharist. These are "cultic" in the sense that through these ritualized acts of worship the Christian comes in vital contact with the priestly act of Jesus' death-resurrection (cf. Rom 6:3-5) or one experiences the prophetic proclamation of his death-resurrection (I Cor 11:26). This cultic aspect of the sacraments and an accelerating interpretation of the Eucharist in sacrificial categories provide one of the bases for later (i.e., post-New Testament) adoption of priestly terminology for the leader of the Eucharist.

It is not certain whether leadership in these cultic acts during the New Testament period was performed by a uniquely designated minister. Various individuals are said to perform baptism (e.g., Paul and Apollos in I Cor 1:12-17; Philip in Acts 8:38), and the Twelve, are commissioned to baptize (Mt 28:18). But we cannot be sure this was the special prerogative of these individuals or groups.

There are no New Testament texts which clearly designate the leader of the Eucharist. In Lk 22:19 Jesus tells the Apostles to "do this in remembrance of me" but we cannot be sure this refers to their being the leaders of the Eucharist or that this

---

[6]Cf., the decrees of Vatican II, *Presbyterorum Ordinis*, 2 and *Lumen Gentium*, 10.

was their exclusive prerogative. The Didache (Ch. 10) refers to prophets as leaders of the Eucharist.[7] Since the Eucharist was an act of proclamation (cf. I Cor 11:26), many scholars suggest that in the earliest period the prophets were the ordinary ministers of the Eucharist.

However, the connection of the Eucharist with the building up and maintaining of the community suggests that presiding at the Eucharist was also performed by the presbyter/bishop. If the priest/bishop of the second and third centuries was the successor to the presbyter/bishop of the late New Testament period, this would explain the clear assignment of cultic leadership to the priest/bishop in such a short time after the New Testament period.

We should keep in mind the possibility that clear restriction of the role of leadership of Eucharist to a designated minister may not have been a concern in the earliest Church. Paul, for example, in two long passages on the Eucharist is quite emphatic about the quality of the community's communal worship but does not mention the presider (see: I Cor 10:14-22; 11:17-34).

2) *The ministry of leadership in the early Church took a variety of forms—later many of them were combined in the offices of presbyter/episkopos.*

As we have suggested above, functions later combined into the role of priest/bishop were likely to have been shared by a number of distinct roles (and/or individuals) in the New Testament period. Also various types of structures may have existed in different local churches or regions, with greater standardization occurring towards the end of the New Testament period. There is some evidence that the Philippian Church, for example (cf. Phil 1:1), may have had a *Presbyteros-episkopos* structure in place at an early period while at Corinth this role was filled by Paul himself as Founding or Missionary Apostle. By the end of the century Corinth, too, had given

---

[7]As R. Brown points out (see, *Critical Meaning of the Bible,* p. 143) the Didache probably appears at a time (around 100 A.D.) when the transition to the bishop and presbyters as leaders in the community is taking place; see Didache 15:1-2 where the community is urged to appoint for itself "bishops and deacons."

way to a presbyter/bishop structure, although with some difficulty.[8] It is impossible to say whether the Philippian structure or the Corinthian structure was more common in the local churches, even those evangelized by Paul.

The functions later assumed by the priest/bishop office obviously include more than cultic leadership. Some of the New Testament ministries that seem to have been absorbed or replaced by this later ministry would be the following:

a) *The "Twelve" or Founding-Apostles:* The origin and function of the "Twelve" are debated. A majority of scholars seems to hold for the choice of the Twelve during Jesus' lifetime as a special group among the disciples. Their number obviously had significance for the eschatological restoration of Israel and is connected with the ultimate purpose and definitive character of Jesus' mission to gather the lost sheep of Israel into a new community (cf. Lk 22:30).

Although Matthew and Mark give a missionary role to the Twelve and designate them as "Apostles" (cf. Mt 10:2; Mk 6:7-13), there is no other indication in the New Testament that members of the Twelve—other than Peter—exercised a missionary role or founded local churches.

It is primarily Luke who focuses on this group as the "Twelve Apostles." In Luke-Acts the Twelve Apostles form a unique group or collegium and in the period after the resurrection provide continuity between Jesus and the early Jerusalem community. One of the first actions taken by the leadership of the community is to reconstitute the Twelve by filling the void left by Judas' defection (Acts 1:15-26). The Risen Christ commissions them to be proclaimers of the gospel and witnesses (Lk 24:45-49). According to the early chapters of Acts, the main function of the Twelve Apostles was to serve as the core group of the Jerusalem Church. Except for Peter (cf. Acts 10) there is little evidence for the missionary activity of the Twelve Apostles. They do have a collegial role in formulating policy decisions affecting the entire Church (e.g., Acts 15:6, 22), but there is no evidence that they founded local

---

[8]This state of affairs is reflected in the Letters of Clement.

churches or set up local leadership. Later legends concerning the travels of the Twelve Apostles and their connection with some local churches have no biblical and apparently little historical basis.

As a college of disciples, bound together by their common witness to Jesus, and their important founding role in the Church, the institution of the "Twelve" has a rich theological meaning. Their witness to the intent and character of Jesus' ministry is an anchor for the community's future. Their care for the Church continues Jesus' own guiding strength in the midst of the community's expanding mission. As unique witnesses to the historical Jesus and his death and resurrection, the Twelve are, in a certain sense, a unique founding group, without successors. But as a symbol of guiding pastoral care entrusted to the Church by the Risen Christ, they are the first and pristine model of a succession of apostolic leaders charged with the Spirit-filled guidance or oversight of the churches.

b) *Missionary Apostles:* These would-be missionaries such as Paul, Barnabas, and Apollos were commissioned to preach the Word and to form new communities. The ministry of the Word is key for this type of "apostle" but they also exercised a degree of authority over local communities or regions (offering instruction, exercising judgments, appointing local leaders, etc.). They may have exercised leadership in worship but this is not certain. They apparently baptized, although Paul does not consider this his prime function (I Cor 1:17). From Paul's letters (particularly references to the collection, to his conferral with Jerusalem leaders, and his overall strategy) it is clear that he, at least, considered relationship to the whole Church also a part of his apostolic responsibility.

However the areas of "jurisdiction" for these missionary apostles were apparently somewhat informal and had vague boundaries. For example, Apollos, Cephas and Paul all seemed to have followings in the Corinthian communities. And in Galatia, Paul was plagued with the incursion of other leading apostles invading his territory.

From indications in the Pastoral Letters, it is likely that the early generation of missionary apostles was replaced by presbyter/bishops in the latter part of the New Testament era, some of them probably appointed by the missionary apostles themselves.

c) *Presbyteros:* The term *presbyteros* or "elder" in its root meaning is a designation of status, not a role. Some recent scholarship, therefore, asserts the New Testament term refers simply to a group of "elders" in the community who through their wisdom and status exercised some informal corporate leadership in the community. It is much more likely, however, that it is used as a quasi-technical term for a role or order in the Church and not just a designation of age or status.

Pastoral care for the community seems to have been the general function of the presbyters and was probably exercised collectively. In most instances, the term appears in the plural and the Pastorals (e.g., I Tim 5:17; Titus 1:5) as well as Acts (11:30; 14:23; 15:2, 4, 6, 22, 23; 16:4; 20:17; 21:18) and I Pet 5:1-2 infer that in many of the local churches a group of presbyters or "elders" was entrusted with the leadership of the community. The term itself probably derives from Judaism and from synagogue organization, although it is also used in the Gentile churches so that elders were found throughout the Church during the New Testament period.[9]

There is undoubtedly a close connection between *presbyteros* and *episkopos;* the terms are used interchangeably in the Pastoral Letters (see below). There is no New Testament evidence to relate the presbyters to cultic leadership. Nor does the later relationship of the presbyterate as the subordinates and extensions of the single bishop seem to have been firmly in place during the New Testament period.

d) *Episkopos:* The noun form of the word *episkopein* ("to oversee") appears five times in the New Testament (Acts 20:28; Phil 1:1; I Tim 3:2; Tit 1:7; I Pet 2:25 [referring to Christ]). In two passages the term *episkopos* seems to be equivalent to and interchangeable with *presbyteros* (cf. Acts 20:28 [previously addressed as "elders" in 20:17]; Titus 1:5, 7). The Pastorals speak of *episkopos* in the singular and *presbyteros* in the plural. It is likely that by the time of the Pastorals, the

[9]R. Brown, *The Critical Meaning of the Bible*, pp. 139-41.

episkopos was chosen from among the elders for special duties of leadership and administration in the local community. There is no clear evidence in the New Testament for the subordination of the presbyterate to a single "overseer," as will be the case in the late second and third century.

Texts referring to the *episkopos* speak of the *requirements* for office (I Tim 3:1-7; Titus 1:7-9) rather than the functions of the office. However, from these qualifications it may be inferred that the main functions of the *episkopos* were administrative oversight and pastoral care (teaching, judging, representing, guiding, etc.). The fact that the *episkopos* was responsible for the overall good of the community suggests that the *episkopos* was also the leader of cult even during the New Testament period, though no texts confirm this. Immediately after the New Testament period, of course, leadership of the Eucharist is a primary role of the *episkopos*.

Note that this office, too, probably had a Jewish origin. Although the term *episkopein* is Greek, the office of "overseer" (*mebaqqar*) in the Qumran community has convinced many recent scholars that this office of pastoral care was adapted by the early Church from Judaism, just as the office of presbyter or elders (*zeqenim*) was adapted from synagogue organization.[10]

e) Other ministerial roles and/or functions were later attributed solely to the bishop in early patristic times but were apparently performed by a variety of individuals in the New Testament community: e.g., *prophet, teacher, scribe* (see Mt 13:52; 23:34) *celebrant of Eucharist* (if this was, in fact, a designated role).

These New Testament "offices" or pastoral leadership roles undergo development and reconfiguration as the early Church settled into the post-apostolic age.

3) *In surveying the various ministries in the early Church, one can make a general distinction between "charismatic" and "institutional" ministries.*

One other general observation that can be made about the

---

[10]Cf., R. Brown, *Priest and Bishop,* pp. 67-68.

exercise of pastoral leadership in the New Testament period—
and one with some importance for a contemporary theology
of priesthood—is the evidence of two basic styles of leadership
in the early decades of the Church. The college of the Twelve,
local Church leaders such as James and his elders, or the
presbyter/episkopos of the later Pauline churches reflect a
more stable or *institutional* form of leadership. On the other
hand, references to itinerant missionaries who preached in the
various communities, prophets endowed with extraordinary
charisms of tongues or teaching, and, to some extent, the
missionary apostles themselves point to a type of *charismatic*
leadership, less bound to the structure of the local Church yet
having some legitimate authority in the proclamation of the
Gospel.[11]

A figure such as the missionary apostle Paul seems to bridge
both forms of leadership—fulfilling a more charismatic function vis-à-vis the Jerusalem Church (and creating some tension
on that account as in his famous confrontation with Peter
over the issue of table fellowship with Gentiles) and a more
institutional form of leadership vis-à-vis some of his own
churches (e.g., Corinth). The itinerant preachers may have
patterned their lifestyle on that of Jesus and his first disciples,
thereby eschewing wealth and assuming the right to hospitality
from the local Christian communities they visited (e.g.,
Mt. 10:8-15). Some scholars speculate that such itinerants were
an important means of preserving the radical sayings of Jesus
on discipleship. At the same time there is evidence, even in the
Gospels themselves, that the ecstatic gifts of the charismatic
leaders were a source of tension with the more established
leaders.[12]

---

[11]On the role of charismatic leadership in the early church, see particularly David E.
Aune, *Prophecy in Early Christianity and the Ancient Mediterranean World* (Grand
Rapids: Eerdmans, 1983), esp. pp. 201-17; and David Hill, *New Testament Prophecy*
(Atlanta: John Knox Press, 1979). See literature on this: Aune, Hill, etc.

[12]Such texts as Mt 7:21-23 might reflect such tension: "Not every one who says to
me, 'Lord, Lord,' shall enter the kingdom of heaven, but he who does the will of my
Father who is in heaven. On that day many will say to me, 'Lord, Lord, did we not
prophesy in your names, and cast out demons in your name, and do many mighty
works in your name?' And then will I declare to them, 'I never knew you; depart from
me, you evildoers.'" See further, D. Aune, *Prophecy in Early Christianity*, pp. 204-205.

These two fundamental strains of leadership—both important for the vitality of the early Church—are sustained in the post-apostolic period through the charismatic institutions of the hermitical movement and later monasticism in their relationship to the institutional structures of the bishop and the local presbyterate. The differing dynamics and functions of such charisms in the apostolic Church are sustained today in the interrelationship of diocesan and religious priesthood. No sound theology can afford to overlook the different expressions these two forms of priesthood have.

Conclusion

This review of the evidence suggests that many of the dominant functions carried out by a variety of ministerial roles in the New Testament period were combined in the single office of bishop (and by extension to his presbyterate) in the post-New Testament period. These would include: the functions of local community care (missionary-apostle, elder, episkopos, deacons [in some churches, e.g., Phoebe at Cenchreae; Rom 16:1-2], pastors [Eph 4:11]), responsibility to the larger Church (founding-apostle, missionary-apostle, itinerant preachers, evangelists), leadership of cult (prophet, possibly missionary-apostle and episkopos), prophecy and teaching (prophets, teachers, scribes).

This process of consolidation had probably already begun in the latter part of the New Testament period (at least by the time of the Pastorals and Johannine Letters) and may have been more advanced in some churches earlier in the first century.

Apostolic Succession

If the above scenario for the development of the office of presbyter/bishop has any validity, it obviously calls for a renewed understanding of "apostolic succession," a point readily admitted by most Catholic scholars today.[13] Apostolic

---

[13]Cf. the discussion of this point in *Interface* (volume 1, Spring 1979, pp. 2-3), a quarterly publication of the Bishops' Committee for Ecumenical and Interreligious Affairs.

succession cannot mean nor does Roman Catholic teaching hold for a direct "physical" or "tactile" continuity from Jesus to the Twelve Apostles to the bishops to the priests and so on. A close look at the New Testament data makes such a scenario impossible (e.g., there is no evidence that the Twelve Apostles appointed any local Church leaders as Paul, an "apostle" who was *not* a member of the Twelve, did). However, from a Catholic perspective this does not mean that the notion of apostolic succession has to be abandoned. Catholic tradition would take note of the following:

a) From the many possible structures of authority that might have emerged from the New Testament or apostolic period, the one that did emerge dominant by the second century was, in fact, the hierarchical model. This development can be seen as a work of the Spirit within the ongoing historical dimension of the Church.

b) Although the fully developed hierarchical model of the second and third centuries is admittedly different from earlier (i.e., varied and less structured) models during the New Testament period, the roots of the hierarchical model can be traced to the New Testament itself.

c) While there is some terminological and structural discontinuity between the New Testament period and later developments, there are also *functional* similarities and underlying historical and theological evolution (e.g., the connection between the missionary apostles of some local churches, the *presbyteros/episkopos* of the Pastorals, and the later bishop and presbyterate/priests of the patristic era).

d) Accepting the legitimacy of development within the Church and viewing the process from the perspective of faith, this evolution can be seen as the work of the Spirit. As R. Brown concludes: "The affirmation that the episcopate was divinely established or established by Christ himself can be defended in the nuanced sense that the episcopate generally emerged in a Church that stemmed from Christ and that this emergence was (in the eyes of faith) guided by the Holy Spirit."[14]

[14]Cf. R. Brown, *Priest and Bishop,* p. 73; on this point, see further, N. Mitchell, *Mission and Ministry,* pp. 207-23.

This line of thinking is analogous to the way one can understand the basic Christian tenet that "Christ founded the Church." This does not have to mean that Jesus of Nazareth in his historical ministry explicitly set in place all the structures of the Church (a proposal that meets grave difficulties in analyzing the New Testament evidence). But one can defend Christ's institution of the Church if this term includes not only the role of historical Jesus in inaugurating the Church in his gathering of disciples to share in his redemptive mission, but also the activity of the Risen Christ and his Spirit at work in the formative circumstances and decisions of the post-resurrection period.[15]

Some conclusions for the theology of priesthood today:

1. The evolution of the priesthood and its diverse forms over the centuries are, in fact, rooted in the biblical data. The Order of Presbyter finds its ultimate foundation in the priestly ministry of Jesus Christ who with compassion gave his own life for the life of the world. It finds affirmation and its ecclesial context in the priestly service of the baptized who through faith in Jesus offer their own lives in compassion and service for the sake of the Reign of God.

While the ministry of the presbyter or priest has a common basis in the redemptive ministry of Jesus, that ministry takes on various expressions in different times and circumstances. The New Testament witnesses to profound changes in the Church's patterns of ministry and order even within the first few decades of the community's existence. Diversity existed not only among the churches but over time and even within a particular category of ministry (e.g., the role of "deacon" described in Acts 6:1-5, namely distributing food rather than preaching, is quite different from what Stephen the "deacon" actually does in Acts 6:8-7:60 and from the responsibility Phoebe seems to have in a Pauline Church [Rom 16:1-2]).

In other words, turning to our biblical heritage does not

---

[15]On this whole question cf. K. Rahner, *The Church and the Sacraments* (Quaestiones Disputatae 9). Herder & Herder, 1963.

provide us with a fixed and static notion of ordained ministry
but a supple and adaptable ministry capable of many different
expressions within the Church.

2. The clear fact that the role of presbyter/ bishop emerged
in the post-New Testament period as a combination of various
roles that previously had existed separately should give us
some perspective on what is happening today when various
functions are, for a number of reasons, being uncoupled from
the role of the priest and redistributed to other ministers.
Adaptation of the priesthood to the current needs of the
Church and realignment due to interrelationship with other
ministries and charisms in the community is not a new
phenomenon, but reflects the state of Church ministry from its
inception.

No single office in the New Testament community—not
even such key roles as the Twelve or Missionary Apostles—
worked in isolation or with complete dominance over other
roles and functions. Leadership in the Jerusalem Church was
somehow shared among the Twelve, James and the elders, and
the deacons. Paul, although fully conscious of his authority as
Apostle, constantly interacted with a myriad of other Christian
leaders and ministers such as the "elders," "deacons," "co-
workers", "fellow apostles," "helpers" mentioned in a single
paragraph of greeting in Romans 16! Christian ministry is by
its nature collaborative and this is a clear and powerful testimony of the New Testament itself.

While perhaps not offering clarity to today's priests and
bishops, awareness of our history can offer perspective and
some serenity in the midst of change.

3. The fundamental distinction between charismatic and
institutional forms of ministry found in the New Testament is
another important historical precedent for expressions of
priesthood today. The differences in style and spirituality that
mark priesthood as expressed in religious life as distinct from
diocesan priesthood are not a recent phenomenon, nor can
these mutually related impulses in the community be ignored
in forging an adequate theology of priesthood.

5. The New Testament's apparent lack of concern with who
presided at the Eucharist might offer us some important per-

spective for our present concerns about priestly identity. This is not to imply that the issue of the priest's identity and the connection of that identity to his unique sacramental function are invalid questions. However, for us, as for Paul in I Corinthians, the primary question for the Church must be the accessibility of the Eucharist to all Christians and the quality of that Eucharistic celebration.

Put in broader New Testament terms, the priesthood that derives from the sacrament of Orders is essentially linked to and draws its essential spirit from the two forms of priesthood mentioned in the Scriptures: the high priesthood of Jesus and the priesthood of the baptized. Only when the three forms of priesthood are linked can a sound theology of ordained priesthood and a proper concern for identity emerge.[16]

[16]"As the Church faces the problem of interrelating its three priesthoods, I foresee struggle in the next twenty years about the role of the ordained priesthood, a struggle both for those already ordained and for those preparing for ordination. Yet, when critically analyzed, the biblical insights about the three priesthoods should enable us, in this period that will lead us into the third millennium, to put the ordained priesthood in a very positive perspective. Always first for us will be the priesthood of Jesus Christ himself, as we come to appreciate more sensitively that we owe him an obedience owed to no other. We shall come to that millennium as part of a Christian people more conscious than ever of its status as a royal priesthood and a holy nation—priestly and holy in lives offered to God which are valuable in the service of the Church—a people conscious that while an ordained ministry of bishop, priest and deacon is necessary for the functioning of the Church, it does not make the ordained any higher in God's sight than he is already being a member of the priesthood of all believers through baptism. And yet, we will still be a Catholic people proud that it continues to call its ministers "priests," because their role in the eucharist is distinctive through the example they give by the sacrifice of their lives, and because by their willingness to surrender themselves to God's will they offer a model of the general priesthood that all share." R. Brown, *The Critical Meaning of the Bible,* pp. 105-106.

Elements for a Theology of Priesthood in the Teaching of the Fathers of the Church

Agnes Cunningham, S.S.C.M.

The teaching of the early Church Fathers on the nature, the functions and the responsibilities of Christian priesthood comes to us in at least three ways. In the first place, it is possible to examine the vocabulary used to speak of priesthood in the patristic era.[1] Secondly, a composite, that is, a general picture of Christian priesthood in the early Christian centuries can be derived from multiple texts in the writings of the Fathers. Finally, a more focused study can be made of several selected documents which specifically address the nature, the functions and the responsibilities of those called to priesthood in the Christian community.

In the following pages, I shall investigate each of these areas: the vocabulary of priesthood; selected texts from the patristic era; significant documents from both the Eastern (St. John Chrysostom and St. Gregory Nazianzen) and the Western (St. Augustine and St. Gregory the Great) traditions.[2] Out of this study, I hope to identify the theological elements or

---

[1] The patristic age dates from Clement of Rome (c. A.D. 95) to Gregory the Great (+ A.D. 604) in the West and John Damascene (+ A.D. 759) in the East.

[2] The documents referred to are: *De sacerdotio,* St. John Chrysostom; *Apologeticus de fuga,* St. Gregory Nazianzen; *Liber Regulae Pastoralis,* St. Gregory the Great. St. Augustine's teaching, while rich and valuable, is not found in any one work. His thought has been studied and presented by Cardinal Michele Pellegrino in, *The True Priest: The Priesthood as Preached and Practiced by St. Augustine* (Philosophical Library, 1968).

principles which seem to characterize the manner in which our Fathers in the faith understood what it meant to exercise priesthood as a ministry in and with Jesus Christ.

The Vocabulary

The early Christian community inherited from the New Testament words which were used to speak of ministers in the *ekklesia.* The first to consider is *presbyteros,* that is, presbyter. When used as a substantive, this world originally meant a person regarded as venerable, because of years or rank. Hence, it could be used to speak of an old person, a veteran or a teacher.[3]

In terms of Christian ministry, according to Lampe's *Patristic Greek Lexicon,*[4] early writers retained the notion of one who was considered as venerable and to be respected. The *presbyteros* (presbyter) was also understood to be one who exercised authority in the Church, although the term could be used when speaking of any respected member of the Christian community. At any rate, the notion of age was not necessarily absent from the use of this word. Indeed, the association of age and office seems to have continued even after the word was used to speak of the presbyter in the tripartite ministry.

However, a certain confusion in meaning can be noted in some early patristic texts. Thus, in some instances, the word used in the New Testament was perceived as Greek in form

---

[3]Reverend Charles Meyer of Mundelein Seminary, University of St. Mary of the Lake adds further precision of meaning: I. As an intransitive verb, *presbeyo* means: 1. to be older, or the eldest; from it derives the word *presbyteros,* from which we have the word, "priest"; 2. to take the place of others, properly by right of seniority; to take precedence. II. As a transitive verb: 1. to place in rank as the oldest; to put first in rank; 2. passively, to have the advantage; to hold the first place; to have the best of it. III. To be an ambassador; to treat or negotiate as one; (Med.) to send ambassadors; or to go as an ambassador.

In Ep 6:20 ("For the sake of this gospel I am an ambassador."), the phrase, "I am an ambassador," translates the Greek word, *presbeyo.* See the excellent article, "*Presbytérat,*" Paul Lamarche, in *Dictionnaire de Spiritualité* LXXX-LXXXI-LXXXII, 2070-2106; Paris Beauchesne, 1985.

[4]Cf. also, H.G. Liddell-R. Scott, *A Greek-English Lexicon.* A new edition revised and augmented by H. St. Jones. Oxford, 1925-1940 (2 vols.).

only. Its meaning was understood to derive from the Jewish institutions of the Old Testament, carrying some type of authority and superiority. The presbyter, or elder, was not meant to be a "mediator." Therefore, he exercised no priestly functions. Presbyters (*presbyteroi*) constituted a "college" in the Church, like the ancients of Israel, before and after the Exodus (cf. Ex 3:16; 4:29). At times, they were seen as members of an "order" who held apostolic power through inheritance or delegation.

The question of apostolic power points to another meaning of the word when *presbyteros* (presbyter) indicated the member of a higher order in a twofold ministry. In other words, the *presbyteros* (presbyter) could be an *episkopos* (overseer, hence: bishop) or a *presbyteros* (presbyter) in references to a *presbyteros* (presbyter) and a *diakonos* (deacon). The close relationship and even identification of the *episkopos* (bishop) and the *presbyteros* (presbyter) can be understood when we recognize the strong association with *paradosis* (Tradition)[5] of the apostolic teaching that was attributed to the *presbyteros* (presbyter).

The word, *presbyteros* (presbyter), is clearly central to an understanding of priesthood, as that concept developed in the patristic age. However, there are several other terms to be considered in a review of significant terminology. One of these is *hiereus* (priest). Once again, we find a diversity of meanings attached to this term. At times, it is synonymous with *presbyteros* (presbyter), although it was used commonly to refer to both *episkopoi* (bishops) and *presbyteroi* (presbyters) in the responsibilities of offering sacrifice and showing pastoral care.

The *hiereus* (priest) was to preside at the celebration of the Eucharist and to exercise functions which might be compared to those of a king. Teaching and holiness of life were expected of the *hiereus* (priest). In those instances where the *hiereus* (priest) was the assistant to the bishop, for example, in the

---

[5]Irenaeus of Lyon uses *paradosis* to speak of the Apostolic Tradition (*Traditio*) in the Church. The role and functions of the bishop in early Christianity are treated at length in the article, "Evêque," F. Prat, in *Dictionnaire de théologie catholique* V, 1656-1701; Paris; 1913. Henceforth, *DTC*.

administration of baptism, the word designated not a *pres-byteros* (presbyter), but a *diakonos* (deacon). In other words, the meaning of *hiereus* (priest) in patristic texts could signify anyone in what came to be known as the *major orders.*[6]

The word *episkopos* (bishop) has already been referred to above. In itself, the term could indicate an overseer, a watcher, or a guardian. the Athenians used the word to designate an inspector sent to supervise a subject state. Hence, it could also refer to a scout or someone assigned to keep watch.

As a word in the vocabulary of the Christian community, *episkopos* (bishop) could be understood in two ways. The *episkopos* (bishop) meant either the bishop or the presbyter, when his ministry was spoken of in relation to that of the *diakonos* (deacon). In texts addressing the tripartite ministry, *episkopos* (bishop) referred solely to the bishop, the overseer of the Church, serving with others: *presbyteroi* (presbyters), *diakonoi* (deacons). With the second century, we see the passage from a local college of "presbyters"—*episkopoi* (bishops), under the direction of an apostle or his disciple, to a college of presbyters under an *episkopos* (bishop), who has inherited "apostolic power."

The second century was marked by diversity and uncertainty in the use of meaning of ministerial titles. There were itinerant ministers known as apostles, prophets and teachers. There were ministers of the community known as *episkopoi* (bishops) and *diakonoi* (deacons). Recent research suggests that the last two titles were commonly used in the Christian communities derived from paganism, while the term, *presbyteroi* (presbyters), prevailed in Jewish-Christian communities.[7]

Toward the end of the second century, a dramatic change in the vocabulary of ministry reflected an underlying change in the concept of priesthood. Most second-century authors had resisted the temptation to present *presbyteroi* (presbyters) as

---

[6]The term "major orders" refers to the episcopacy, the priesthood and the diaconate. This term is no longer used in Catholic teaching on the Sacrament of Orders.

[7]*The First Epistle of Clement to the Corinthians,* 40, 5. Ancient Christian Writers, 1. James A. Kleist, S.J., trans. and ann. Westminster, Maryland: The Newman Bookshop, 1946.

mediators. They had had no desire to apply the term, *hiereus* (priest), to the Christian minister, in order to avoid continuity with the concepts of the Old Testament. However, Old Testament terminology was progressively introduced into the works of Christian authors. The priestly vocabulary of the Old Testament came to be applied commonly to the ministers of the Christian community.

One reason for this seems to have been the need to claim the Old Testament as the Christian Scriptures. This was done through a Christological reading of the Law and the Prophets as well as through commentaries on and exegesis of the Sacred Writings. The foundations of the Christian gospel were in the Word of God. Thus, the titles—high priest, priest, levite—given to Christian ministers indicated the fulfillment of what was foretold in Israel.

On another level, as Greek was replaced by Latin in the Roman Empire and, consequently, in Christianity, the vocabulary of ministry was necessarily affected. The Latin equivalent of *presbyteros* (presbyter) can be presumed to be *sacerdos.* The term would be used, in some instances, to refer to both the *episkopos* (bishop) and the *presbyteros* (presbyter). The *episkopos* (bishop), as *sacerdos,* was known as the *vicarius Christi* or, even, as the *"ecclesia."* The *presbyteroi* (presbyters) were *sacerdotes secundi ordinis.* The term *sacerdotium* came to designate priesthood in a general sense. *Sacerdos* would still carry the earlier meaning attributed to presbyter. Soon, however, *sacerdos* took on the sense of *hiereus* (priest) in its application to Christian priesthood. This development was related to the significance of still another Latin term.

The word, *clerus,* was first used to refer to the entire body of the faithful. They were the "inheritance" of the Lord (Ps 28:9; Ps 33:12). As early a *I Clement,* that is, prior to the emergence of a Latin Christian vocabulary, a distinction had been made between the laity and the clergy. In time, *clerus* came to signify all those *"qui in ecclesiastici ministerii gradibus ordinati sunt."*[8] Nonetheless, the tradition of the early Christian centuries

---

[8]This widely-quoted phrase has been attributed to Theophanes, *Homily XII*, 70.

prevailed in the conviction that *all* members of the *ekklesia* share in the authentic priesthood of Jesus Christ.[9]

This brief review of the vocabulary associated with priesthood in the early Christian community points to the fact that development was a characteristic of the concept of ministry from the beginning. That development accounted, on the one hand, for an amazing diversity. For example, during the episcopacy of Cornelius in Rome (A.D. 251-253), in addition to the bishop, there were 46 presbyters, 7 deacons, 7 sub-deacons, 42 acolytes and 52 exorcists, readers and doorkeepers. It reminds us, on the other hand, that as the Church continues to grow in understanding the rich dimensions and significance of that priesthood which is rightly known as Christian, the vocabulary and terminology of the concept will both reflect and influence development, as they did in the patristic era. This development can be perceived not only in the changing vocabulary of ministry, but also in the reflections and exhortations found in the writings of many of the Fathers who sought to express their deep convictions and understandings regarding priesthood in the Church.

The Teaching of the Fathers

It is not possible to find a systematic, "ordered" doctrine concerning the presbyterate in the writings of the Fathers of the Church. The teaching of the Fathers, however, does address the nature of the presbyterate, along with the functions and responsibilities of those Christians who exercised that ministry.[10]

The documents of the Ante-Nicene era refer to the *presbyteroi* (presbyters) as ministers appointed to an "order" founded on the Will of Christ and the apostles (I Clement).

---

[9]Cf. article "Priest" in *The Oxford Dictionary of the Christian Church*, Second Edition. F. L. Cross and E. A. Livingstone, eds. London: Oxford University Press, 1974, p. 1123.

[10]I have relied on several articles for the material in this section. Cf. *DS*, "Presbytérat" (LXXX, LXXXI, LXXXII), "Sacerdoce" (XCI); *DTC* "Evêque" (V), "Ordre" (XI), "Prêtre" (XIII).

They were endowed with spiritual authority (Shepherd of Hermas). They were to receive and faithfully transmit the *Traditio,* thus assuring unity in the *ekklesia* through their own oneness with the apostolic teaching (Irenaeus). Both the *episkopos* (bishop) and the *presbyteros* (presbyter) were bound to the priesthood of Christ: the *episkopos* (bishop), fully; the *presbyteros* (presbyter), in a complementary manner.

Later writers, reflecting the changing terminology and concept of the age, developed this theme of participation in the priesthood of Christ. The presbyters (*sacerdotes*) of the *ekklesia* were to be with Christ. The Fathers are unanimous in proclaiming Christ as the true and only *hiereus* (priest) of the New Covenant. Most frequently, Christ is spoken of as the "High Priest" (Caesarius of Arles; Eusebius of Pamphili; Basil of Caesarea; Clement of Alexandria). His priesthood is not and cannot be repeated. However, Christ's priesthood becomes the "model" and *typos* (type) of Christian priesthood. For this reason, the figure of Melchizedek emerges as significant, since the sacrifice of Christ was prefigured in that of the King of Salem (Cyprian of Carthage; Justin Martyr; Gregory of Nyssa; Cyril of Jerusalem; Ambrose of Milan). Thus, Christian priesthood is both royal and prophetic because of Christ, the anointed of God, prophet, king, priest.

As priest, Christ was anointed to be a priest forever. He is to be considered the archetype, in whom the fullness of the priesthood is to be found. The multiple references that compare Christ's priesthood to that of Melchizedek are careful to distinguish Christ as priest from the priests of the Old Testament. The major points of similarity between Christ and Melchizedek lie in the prophetic nature of a sacrifice that is unbloody and the eternity that is assured through fidelity to an anointing.

Christian ministers[11] were to understand their priesthood in terms of the whole community of the faithful, that is, as a participation in the saving mission of the Church in history.

---

[11]The term, ministers, is used here to highlight the lack of clarity in the use of *presbyteros* (presbyter), *episkopos* (overseer, bishop), *hiereus* (priest).

As a result, their priesthood was linked to the Eucharist (Ambrose; Caesarius of Arles). This is realized, primarily, through the offering of a sacrifice which is meant to be both visible and invisible. The *presbyteros* (presbyter)/*sacerdos*, like Christ, is to be both priest and victim (Peter Chrysologus). The meaning of Eucharist in the life of the priest brings together the Christian mysteries of the chalice, the death of Christ, and a life of witness or martyrdrom (Origen).

The functions of the *presbyteros* (presbyter) in early Christianity were defined in terms of the meaning this word carried. The earliest known patristic texts are the *First Epistle to the Corinthians*, attributed to Clement of Rome,[12] and the *Letters* of Ignatius of Antioch.[13] Clement's reference to the existence of the tripartite ministry in the Christian community has been, at times, discounted. One reason for this attitude is the unwillingness of some writers to admit the possibility of hierarchical structure this early in the history of the Church. Another reason is the evidence—or lack of evidence—regarding the ecclesiastical organization of the Church of Rome at this period. Still another reason is Clement's use of Jewish terminology for the ministers of whom he speaks. His text reads:

> Special functions are assigned to the high priest;
> a special office is imposed upon the priests; and
> special ministrations fall to the Levites.[14]

There is no convincing reason to doubt Clement's existence, his position as Bishop of Rome, his responsibility as pastor for

---

[12]The text and translation of Clement's *Letter* can be found in the Loeb Classical Library Series, Vol. 1: *The Apostolic Fathers*, K. Lake, New York and London, 1930. The *Letter* is usually dated A.D. 96-98, although some scholars would place it earlier.

[13]Both the authenticity and the number of the *Letters* of Ignatius have been the object of dispute over the centuries. The authenticity of the Ignatian *corpus* is no longer questioned. Scholars today agree that the number is seven; the *Letters* are found in a text, originally in Greek and still extant, known as *the short recension*. Cf. K. Lake, *The Apostolic Fathers*, Vol. 1, Loeb Classical Library, New York and London, 1930.

[14]Cf. I Clement, 40.

other churches. Scholars generally agree that his use of Jewish terminology to refer to ministers in the Christian community is one of several evidences that most probably reveal his Jewish background.[15] We can be reasonably confident that Clement's *hiereus* (priest) is, indeed, a *presbyteros* (presbyter). His brief allusion, however, tells us almost nothing about the specific role or functions of the presbyter in the Church. Indeed, in Clement, the term *episkopos* (bishop) and *presbyteros* (presbyter) seem, in general, to be synonymous.

The Letters of Ignatius of Antioch contain a number of references to the presbyter and his responsibilities in the Christian community. The *presbyteros* (presbyter) is to be a comfort and support to the bishop.[16] With the deacons, the presbyters assure the unity of a church through the assistance and obedience they give to the bishop. They are to be held in respect "as God's high council and as the apostolic college."[17] They are, in fact, representatives of Christ's apostles. In the colorful language that is his, Ignatius describes the company of presbyters as men "appropriately chosen" to work so closely with the bishop that they form a "fittingly woven spiritual crown."[18]

Ignatius perceives the unity of the presbyterate with the bishop and the deacons as the necessary element that assures the integrity and fidelity of the Christian people. Indeed, the unity that exists among the bishop, his presbyters and his deacons is a symbol, for Ignatius, of the God who is One and Three as well as of the one bread and the one cup of the Eucharist, which unites us with the one Flesh and Blood of the Lord Jesus Christ. In Ignatius, we have a clear sense of the presbyter and the place he holds in the life and ministry of the Church.

Several other themes are emphasized by the Fathers, looking to the priesthood of Christ in a desire to understand Christian

[15]Clement is generally regarded as a Greek-educated convert from Judaism.

[16]See, especially, Philadelphians, Smyrnaeans, Trallians.

[17]Trallians, 3.

[18]Magnesians, 13.

priesthood. One of these is the role of Christ as Mediator (Clement of Alexandria). In this capacity, Christ assumes the task of an educator who is to bring God's Truth to humankind. The Christian presbyter is to be a faithful witness to the *paradosis* (Tradition) of the apostles (Eusebius Pamphili; Tertullian; Caesarius of Arles). This implies the importance of preaching as an element of Christian priesthood (Basil of Caesarea; Ambrose of Milan; Jerome; Caesarius of Arles; Clement of Alexandria; Prosper of Aquitaine). Indeed, the fundamental task of the presbyter was seen as the proclamation of the gospel of Jesus Christ (*Didaché*, Irenaeus).

Gregory of Nazianzus, Caesarius of Arles and Leo the Great wanted their presbyters to be educated in the knowledge of religious truth and doctrine. This would enable them to instruct and inspire the faithful. Further, Leo was in favor of "the custom handed down to us," namely, that one to be ordained was to advance through the designated orders. This would enable him to learn "over a long period of time" what he would later teach to others.

As the role of the *episkopos* (bishop) became more clearly distinguished from that of other ministers, so, too, were the functions attributed to each order more clearly identified. From the third century on, ordination rites referred to the tripartite ministry (*Apostolic Tradition*). With the multiplication of *tituli* (parishes) and the expansion of Christianity, especially into rural or remote areas of the empire, presbyters were allowed to exercise functions previously reserved for the *episkopos* (bishop): leadership of local churches; administration of penance and forgiveness of sin; celebration of the Eucharist.

Increasingly, the *episkopos* (bishop) was recognized as a "prince," holding a place in the empire, after Constantine, equal to that of the senators. While the *Didascalia Apostolorum* had affirmed the bishop as "absolute lord," with a subordinate role assigned to the presbyters, monasticism and the increasingly exalted position of the presbyter were reactions to a development that threatened the spiritual values of the priesthood in general.

The primary responsibility of the Christian presbyter was to be a "spiritual man." Ignatius of Antioch proclaimed a mystical theology of the *episkopos* (bishop) as the image of God (Eph 6:1). Throughout the Age of the Martyrs, the spiritual nature of salvation was perceived in its relation to the authority of the bishop and his unity with the people entrusted to his care. Ambrose, Augustine, John Chrysostom and Gregory the Great all claimed and demonstrated in their lives that the spiritual dimension of the episcopate was possible.

Both Eastern and Western writers insisted on the holiness necessary to the *presbyteros* (presbyter), because he was to proclaim the Word, celebrate the Mysteries[19] and lead the community. The *presbyteros* (presbyter) was called to live the demands of his ministry, because of Christ who was priest, mediator and shepherd; because of the Church, which was to be served as the living temple of God and the body of Christ. The holiness of the presbyter was to be found with the community of the faithful, in the ministry of the Word, in contemplation, poverty, charity and apostolic zeal (Gregory the Great). The holiness of the presbyter was related to his mission of mediating reconciliation with Christ's divine nature (Clement of Alexandria). Theodore of Mopsuestia called the priest to live for others "like an angel who leads them to virtue."[20] For Maximus the Confessor (+ A.D. 662), the priest is to be the servant of unity in the Church.

The Fathers did not hesitate to admonish and exhort presbyters who lives did not bear witness to their vocation. Chastity, charity and concern for the poor were to be their preferred virtues (Ambrose). Greed and luxurious living conditions were frequently cited as unworthy of one who was a minister of Christ. So, too, were the desire or ambition for promotion, a contentious, argumentative spirit and the lack of charity, especially toward the poor and the ill. Because a presbyter's position in the Christian community necessarily placed him in a rank above others, he was to "excel" in holiness of life and service, so as to be less unworthy of the respect shown to him.

---

[19]This term was used in the patristic age to refer to those ecclesial actions which especially communicated the presence of God, e.g, the sacraments, especially, the Eucharist.

[20]*Patrologia Graeca (PG)* LVI, 609c.

In his commentary on the Lord's Prayer, Gregory of Nyssa describes the spiritual preparation which Jesus Christ provides for those who are to be ordained to the priesthood:

> He does not manufacture the priestly beauty from alien adornments produced from dyes and curious devices of weaving, but He puts on him his own native adornments, decking him with the graces of virtue rather than with an embroidered purple robe. Not with earthly gold does He adorn his breast, but his very heart He makes beautiful through a perfectly pure conscience. He also fits the diadem with the rays coming from precious stones; they are the lustre of the holy commandments, according to the Apostle ... [T]here He leads him to the *adyton,* that is, to the innermost part of the Temple.[21]

When the Fathers speak to or about the *presbyteros* (presbyter) in the Christian community, it is usually within the context of the tripartite ministry. The relationship of the presbyter to the bishop and the deacons is highlighted. The additional responsibilities of the *episkopos* (bishop) as leader and principal teacher and minister of the community are indicated. However, even in the fourth and fifth centuries, authors like John Chrysostom and Jerome, when discussing the relation between presbyters and bishops, seem to perceive little difference between the two ministries.

A developing theology of priesthood in the patristic era cannot disregard this point. We have seen that, in an earlier age, the *presbyteros* (presbyter) was the bishop's assistant, support, adviser and replacer. As the Church grew in numbers, the presbyter became more important and his services more necessary in the life of the Church, so as to alleviate the tasks and duties assigned to the bishop. It was most important that a serious articulation of the nature, functions and responsibilities of the priesthood be expressed. At least four great Fathers did undertake this task. The documents they have left to the Church are a precious legacy.

[21] *Oratione in diem luminum*; PG XLVI, 581-583.

Toward a Theology of Priesthood

One of the questions frequently asked about priesthood in the patristic age addresses the manner in which a Christian entered this ministry. Did the individual make a free choice of his own? Was he called from and by the community to which he belonged? Was he chosen by some pre-determined, approved manner? There are several ways in which to answer these questions. Clement of Rome has described the process by which men were to be chosen for the office of bishop:

> Our Apostles, too, were given to understand by our Lord Jesus Christ that the office of bishop would give rise to intrigues. For this reason, equipped as they were with perfect foreknowledge, they appointed the men mentioned before, and afterwards laid down a rule once for all to this effect: when these men die, other approved men shall succeed to their sacred ministry.[22]

In other words, bishops and presumably, presbyters, were chosen for an office of service in the Church. This method led, at times, to awkward, embarrassing or difficult situations, when the person chosen was elected against his will. Paschasius of Dumium relates several stories of men ordained unwillingly.

One of the most memorable accounts of an unwilling *ordinand* is that recorded by Gregory of Nazianzus. In his second occasional oration, *Apologeticus de fuga,* Gregory gives us the reasons for his desire to avoid ordination and his explanation for having fled to the desert in order to escape the burdens and responsibilities of priesthood.

Gregory, the son of a bishop, was ordained a presbyter by his father in A.D. 362, about the age of 32. His deep respect and high regard for the priesthood led him to abandon his charge. He did return to Nazianzus and in writing an apology for his flight, he composed what has been considered a treatise on the priesthood, that was used by both John Chrysostom and Gregory the Great in their works on that subject.

Gregory saw the priesthood as a state that called for daring

[22]I Clement, 40-44.

and risk on the part of one who would aspire to it or be chosen for it. One who would offer the Eucharist would have to have hands consecrated "with holy works;" his eyes ought to marvel at the works of the Creator; his ears, "closed to harsh words," were to be open to the counsel of a wise man. In a word, his whole being and every member and faculty of his person were to be "directed toward God" (95).

"Who will take this risk?" Gregory asks. Only one whose heart has been "tested by fire" (96); one who has become the "temple of the living God and the living abode of Christ in the Spirit" (97); one who can "lift up Christ's cross." Gregory's terror at the thought of his inadequacy to be a true priest was tempered by his compunction and humble return to the people he had abandoned. When we realize that he never visited the city (Sasima) for which his friend, Basil of Caesarea, had ordained him bishop and that he had to resign after a brief period as bishop of Constantinople, we can wonder if he ever was able to accept the fact that the priesthood demanded a stature that he was convinced he could not attain:

> For a small man, personal safety lies in carrying a small burden and not subjecting himself to things beyond his ability, thereby bringing ridicule upon himself and at the same time running the added risk, as we have heard, of building a tower that is suitable for no one else than him who has the means to complete it.[23]

While the *Apologeticus de fuga* is not a treatise in the strict sense of the word, it did inspire the first formal treatise on the priesthood in Christian theological writing. St. John Chrysostom wrote the *De Sacerdotio* about A.D. 386. This work, in the form of an imagined dialogue between Chrysostom and a friend, Basil, had two purposes. In the first place, it was meant to justify Chrysostom's actions at the time the two friends were to have been ordained bishops, about A.D. 373. The two agreed to accept ordination, but Chrysostom fled

[23]Epistle I, 156.

after leading Basil to think he had been ordained. Only after his ordination did Basil learn that Chrysostom had tricked him. Secondly, the treatise, in the words of Isidore of Pelusium (+ c. 435), "sets forth how venerable and how difficult is the office of the priesthood," and it shows how to fulfill it as it ought to be fulfilled.

The treatise is comprised of six sections or "books." In book one, Chrysostom relates the incident of the ordination, Basil's expression of anger and hurt at having been deceived by his friend, and the beginning of Chrysostom's defense for his action. The first book closes with this argument:

> He indeed is justly called a deceiver who uses artifice for an unjust end, but not he who acts thus from an upright motive. Yet it is often necessary to practice deception and to derive great advantage thereby, while the man who acts with simplicity has often done great injury to the person whom he has not deceived.[24]

In book two, Chrysostom explains his reasoning further. Basil's qualities, his virtue and great charity were signs of his worthiness for ordination to the fullness of the priesthood as a bishop. Chrysostom was convinced that he himself lacked the greatness and nobility of soul required for the office. For him, it represented great danger and difficulty. The good of Basil and of the people whose shepherd he was to be, required his ordination. Chrysostom, on the contrary, feared that,

> having received the flock of Christ in a healthy and sound condition, I should harm it by my negligence, and draw upon myself the indignation of Him who so loves it, that He delivered Himself up as the price of its salvation.[25]

Chrysostom's thoughts on the greatness of the priesthood are set forth in an admirable passage in book three:

---

[24] *De sacerdotio*, I, 9.
[25] *Ibid.*, II, 4.

The work of the priesthood is done on earth, but it is ranked among heavenly ordinances. And this is only right, for no man, no angel, no archangel, no other created power, but the Paraclete himself ordained this succession, and persuaded men, while still remaining in the flesh, to represent the ministry of angels. The priest, therefore, must be as pure as if he were standing in heaven itself, in the midst of those powers.[26]

Like Elijah, the priest brings down, not fire, but the Holy Spirit so that "grace may descend upon the victim, and through it inflame the souls of all and render them brighter than silver fire-tried" (III, 3).

The power and dignity granted to priests by God cannot be measured, according to Chrysostom, by earthly standards:

It is to priests that spiritual birth and regeneration by baptism is [*sic*] entrusted. By them we put on Christ, and are united to the Son of God, and become members of that blessed head. Hence we should regard them as more august than princes and kings, and more venerable than parents. For the latter begot us of blood and the will of the flesh, but priests are the cause of our generation from God, of our spiritual regeneration, of our true freedom and sonship according to grace.[27]

Outstanding holiness and virtue are required of this minister. He must not be ambitious for worldly honor. Not only the bishop, but also every presbyter is to be prudent, wise and clear-sighted. He must be able to accept insult and blame with patient endurance. Chrysostom looks as well for a combination of piety and intelligence in the one who is to be ordained. He must be ready and prepared to answer the arguments and attacks of the enemies of Christianity, whether they be Jews,

---

[26]*Ibid.*, III, 4.
[27]*Ibid.*, III, 6.

pagans or heretics. Most importantly, he must have the qualifications of a good preacher.

The great gift of preaching and its necessity for the priestly ministry are treated in detail in book five of the treatise. This section of the work has been called "a manual for preachers." Chrysostom describes the labor and diligence required for this task and the difficulties and dangers that face one who would accomplish it worthily. One who would instruct and inspire his hearers must be gifted with "contempt of praise and the force of eloquence." He must be unaffected by applause or criticism; he must be able to teach "with grace, seasoned with salt" (Col 4:6). The preacher must neither heed the praise showered on him nor grow discouraged when it is lacking. The purpose of his discourse must be to please God.

The final book of the treatise is a reflection on the difference between the active life and the contemplative life. There is no comparison, in Chrysostom's eyes, between the dangers and difficulties of the monastic life and those of priestly ministry. The burden of responsibility for others carried by the presbyter requires greater virtue, charity and perfection than what is required of monks. This is reason enough for Chrysostom to feel unequal to the office of bishop.

John Chrysostom's treatise, *De sacerdotio*, has been held in esteem as "a classic on the priesthood and one of the finest treasures of Patristic literature."[28] Although the occasion and subject refer, primarily, to the episcopacy, its teaching has always been regarded as a contribution to the nature and role of priesthood in the Christian community. With the *Apologeticus de fuga* of Gregory of Nazianzus, the *De sacerdotio* translates the theological insights of the Eastern Church in the Golden Age on the subject of priestly life and ministry.

If we look to the West to explore the teaching of the Fathers on priesthood, our attention is drawn, first of all, to Augustine of Hippo (+ A.D. 430). Although Augustine never wrote a

---

[28]Johannes Quasten, *Patrology III*, p. 459. Utrecht/Antwerp: Spectrum Publishers, 1966.

treatise on the priesthood, he did express his thoughts on the subject in many writings, especially in his sermons.

Like Gregory of Nazianzus, Augustine was ordained to the priesthood against his will. In a sermon preached toward the end of his life, Augustine stated:

> I made a practice of never going to any place where I knew the episcopal see to be vacant, since my knowledge that I enjoyed a certain reputation among the servants of God made me mortally afraid of being made a bishop.[29]

Possidius, the author of Augustine's first biography, describes the scene that took place on a visit Augustine made to Hippo. Although the bishop was "in good shape," he took advantage of Augustine's presence to suggest him as successor in the see of Hippo. Possidius writes:

> They [the crowd] laid hold of him and, as was the custom in such cases, presented him to the bishop for ordination, all crying loudly and zealously that so it should be done.[30]

Augustine expressed other sentiments: "Violence was done to me, but I must have merited it by my sins, seeing that I can find no other explanation." He further commented: "I was taken by surprise and made a priest. And this proved to be a stepping-stone to the episcopate."[31]

What was the "true priest" to be, according to this man who became a great theologian, a model bishop, a saint in God's Church? Augustine understood that the priesthood demanded total dedication. The bishop, the preacher, the priest had to "live up to his name." If a man is called by a name that he is not faithful to in his heart, the name will bring him only "an ever greater accumulation of guilt."[32]

---

[29]Pellegrino, *op. cit.*, p. 19.

[30]"Life of St. Augustine by Bishop Possidius," in Fathers of the Church, 15, p. 77; trans., Sister Mary Magdeleine Muller, O.S.F., Ph.D. and Roy J. Defferari, Ph.D. Fathers of the Church Inc., 1952.

[31]Pellegrino, *op cit.*, p. 20.

[32]*Ibid.*, p. 153.

Augustine identifies the qualities and virtues that must characterize a true presbyter: genuineness, humility, Christian love. Pellegrino points out that Augustine shared the opinion of the Church Fathers in general, namely, that "the priesthood is essentially *a social office, consecrating its holder to the service of the Church.*"[33] The obligations a priest holds towards the community are serious; there are to be "no limitations or compromises." In his exclusive consecration to the service of the Church by the exercise of the functions of his ministry, Augustine claimed that the priest was filled with "an unshakable trust and confidence from a strange source." This *source* is the grace of Christ which sustains the vision of the priestly life. Augustine knew he was a bishop—and, first of all, a priest—"by God's gracious decree."

Augustine did not aspire to the priesthood. His visit to Hippo in A.D. 391 was undertaken for the purpose of finding a place to found a monastery in which he could live with his brothers. Once ordained and "consecrated ... in the ministry of the Word and the mystery of God," he devoted himself to liturgical activity, to preaching and writing, to study and prayer. In this way of life, Augustine learned the "Christocentric" nature of the priesthood:

> its origin lies in a divine election; its power comes from the action of Christ himself, whose instrument it is; and its ideal is the service of fellow-Christians for the love of Christ.[34]

With Gregory the Great (+ 604), the Patristic age in the West comes to an end. He served the Church as Bishop of Rome for fourteen years and, as Pope, took for himself the title cherished since then by all Roman Pontiffs: *servus servorum Dei.* It is generally acknowledged that Gregory was inspired by the Nazianzen's *Apologeticus de fuga* to undertake his work on pastoral care, *Liber Regulae Pastoralis.*[35]

---

[33]*Ibid.,* p. 23.

[34]*Ibid.,* p. 149.

[35]For an English translation, see *Pastoral Care,* trans., Henry Davis, S.J. Ancient Christian Writers (*ACW*) II. Westminster, Maryland: The Newman Press, 1950.

Like others before him, Gregory, too, experienced a certain sense of reluctance when he was called from his monastic life for a more public service in the Church. The treatise we are about to consider was a reply to those who admonished him. It deals, primarily, with the responsibilities and burdens of the episcopal office, but also sets forth the dignity and difficulties of the priesthood. Gregory, like the Nazianzen and John Chrysostom, hoped to show how the duties of the priestly office are to be fulfilled.

The *Liber Regulae Pastoralis* is divided into four parts. In part one, Gregory identifies the difficulties of priestly ministry and the requirements necessary to face them. In the second part, Gregory discusses both the interior and the outer life of a good pastor. Since Gregory, like the Fathers in general, looks upon preaching and teaching as an essential part of priestly ministry, he devotes part three to the consideration of that responsibility. The fourth and final section reminds the pastor not to forget his own weaknesses and limitations.

Gregory describes the "character of a man who comes to rule," that is, the person called to be a spiritual leader of others in priesthood. The complete text is worth citing:

> He, therefore—indeed, he precisely—must devote himself entirely to setting an ideal of living. He must die to all passions of the flesh and by now lead a spiritual life. He must have put aside worldly prosperity; he must fear no adversity, desire only what is interior. He must be a man whose aims are not thwarted by a body out of perfect accord through frailty, nor by any contumacy of the spirit. He is not led to covet the goods of others, but is bounteous in giving of his own. He is quickly moved by a compassionate heart to forgive, yet never so diverted from perfect rectitude as to forgive beyond what is proper.... He so studies to live as to be able to water the dry hearts of others with the streams of instruction imparted. By his practice and experience of prayer he has learned already that he can obtain from the Lord what he asks for....[36]

[36] *Pastoral Care* I, 10.

Gregory shows keen insight into human nature and what might be called a "natural sense of human psychology." In his section on preaching, he counsels the priest to give heed to the persons to whom he is speaking and to be aware of their diverse needs because of age, sex, employment, social status, marital state, health, virtue, mood or other differentiating condition. His words reveal the kind of wisdom a spiritual leader ought to desire:

> Often, for instance, what is profitable to some, harms others. Thus, too, herbs which nourish some animals, kill others; gentle hissing that calms horses, excites young puppies; medicine alleviates one disease, aggravates another; and bread such as strengthens the life of robust men, destroys that of little children.[37]

Just because of reflections such as these, Gregory's work remains even today "as a source of knowledge, inspiration, and enlightenment to rulers, pastors in high office or low, preachers and confessors."[38] His final admonition is not to be disregarded: when the preacher [priest, pastor] has done everything required of him, through the functions of his office, he "should return to himself" lest he become proud and betray the life and service to which he has been called.[39]

Concluding Reflections

What conclusions can be drawn from the preceding review of evidences and documents referring to priesthood in the writings of the Fathers of the Church? There seem to be several.

In the first place, as it was indicated earlier, there is no systematic doctrine of priesthood in any of the writings of the patristic era. Perhaps it is not an exaggeration to say that a study of the *Traditio Apostolica* attributed to Hippolytus would uncover the first liturgical elaboration of a theology of

---

[37] *Pastoral Care* III, Prologue.
[38] *ACW*, Introduction, p. 8.
[39] *Pastoral Care* IV.

priesthood, with a definitive, fixed terminology. Such a study did not fall within the limits of this paper.

Secondly, the bond between vocabulary and concept, especially in light of a changing language-frame, must be acknowledged. The shift from Greek to Latin, for example, facilitated the growing awareness in the Christian community of the similarities and differences between Old Testament ideas of priesthood and those identified as proper to Christian priesthood. Developments in this area were also related to changing pastoral needs, along with the social and political adjustments that characterized the status of Christianity in the Constantinian era.

In terms of the functions perceived as appropriate to priesthood, priority must be given to the proclamation of the Word. Presbyters were recognized its teachers. Liturgical leadership, at first reserved to the bishop, was gradually assigned to the presbyter, although the manner and occasion of its exercise were dependent on the mandate and delegation of the bishop. Here, we must note the diversity of practice that prevailed among local churches as well as between Eastern and Western Christianity.

Other presbyteral functions were largely caritative in nature. Care and service of the poor, the sick and the elderly, a spirit of dedication, personal generosity and Christian love were also to be important values in the life of the presbyter.

The Fathers wrote and preached eloquently on the subject of spirituality in the priesthood. Avoidance of luxury, envy, unworthy ambition and every type of immorality was a primary duty for everyone consecrated through ordination to the service of the Church. More importantly, the Fathers clearly described the spiritual values necessary for priesthood and called for a positive commitment to them: prayer, ascesis, charity.

Although the term "contemplation" is not usually mentioned as a specific requirement in the life of the priest, the emphasis placed by all the Fathers on the necessity and importance of prayer, of the interior life and of obedience to the Holy Spirit is worthy of attention. Priesthood called for a man who could be both the one who offered sacrifice and the victim offered, through the spiritual sacrifice of his own life. He was the one through whom Christ could continue his ministry in the Church. For many of the early Fathers, a personal experience of monastic life had convinced them of the need to bring together in their priesthood the values of contemplation and ministerial service.

Still another influence from the monastic tradition was the gradual tendency to recommend both celibacy and the common life for those who were members of the presbyterate. All of these values had their moment, at one time or another, during the patristic era. They were never imposed in that period, but neither did they disappear completely from subsequent discussions of priestly life in later ages.

At certain key moments in the history of the Church, a number of influences came to bear on the developing theological insights regarding Christian priesthood. One such moment occurred at the beginning of the fourth century, with the peace of Constantine, when growing numbers of Christians required changes in pastoral practice for bishops and presbyters. Another took place during the fourth century, when the Church in North Africa suffered such a severe lack of clergy that some local communities did not even have a deacon. In response to the need of the time, monks were ordained as were priests, converts from Donatism.

In the East, there was little, if any, evolution of presbyteral priesthood after the sixth century. In the West, on the contrary, new developments continued in the articulation of a theology and a spirituality of priesthood, especially in the Latin Church. While the East emphasized the dignity of the priest in his communication of the divine action revealed in the Incarnation, the West found the dignity of priesthood to reside in his leadership and the responsibilities he assumed for the observance of disciplinary, liturgical and moral norms.

That development continues today. It is revealed in the awareness of new needs in the Church, of new demands on those ordained to Christian priesthood, in new questions asked about ministry, in attempted answers from many quarters. The Fathers did not ask all the questions being asked today, although they did consider some of them. Time spent reflecting on the teachings that come to us from the patristic age can be profitable, if only as a point of reference and a reminder that the Church in every age is called to fidelity to a *Traditio* that is apostolic because it is living; that remains alive, as long as it is truly apostolic.

Diocesan and Religious Models of Priestly Formation: Historical Perspectives

John O'Malley, S.J.

The topic I have been asked to address in these few pages is difficult for several reasons. First, it is vast, ranging over the full two millennia of the history of Christianity. Secondly, although we possess a few scattered monographs treating certain aspects of it, it has never been studied in an adequate and systematic way. There does not exist in any language, for instance, a comprehensive *History of the Seminary* on an international basis.[1] The situation for the training of members of religious orders and congregations has been even more assiduously neglected. Thirdly, the documentation that survives pertains largely to the genre of edifying literature, which exacerbates the problem of interpretation. Just imagine, for instance, trying to reconstruct what goes on in seminaries today from fund-raising brochures published in their honor! The more serious studies, moreover, tend to deal with institutional issues like curriculum, finances, faculty training, and number of students, and do not penetrate to the deeper issues of religious culture, religious anthropology, and ecclesiological assumptions. Finally, I am here standing not on the firm native ground of my academic speciality, but at the insistence of

---

[1] See, e.g., the comments and bibliogrphy in Paul F. Grendler, "Schools, Seminaries, and Catechetical Instruction" in *Catholicism in Early Modern History: A Guide to Research*, ed. John W. O'Malley (St. Louis, 1988), pp. 315-30.

friends, improperly so called, am venturing into alien territory, known to all to be filled with land-mines of massively destructive power.

Under these circumstances about all I can promise to do is to touch on some aspects of the problems that have attracted my attention in my other research and then present to you some of the questions that they raise in my mind about our current situation. I divide what I have to say into three unequal parts: (1) a sweeping review of the historical data as I see it from the twelfth century until Vatican II; (2) a brief analysis of the pertinent documents of the Council; (3) a presentation to you of some issues thus raised in my mind.

As a preamble, however, I must tell you that in my opinion, discussion today of the formation of the diocesan and religious clergy is based on the assumption that we are dealing with essentially the same models. This assumption is based, as we shall see, on solid historical grounding, for we are dealing with institutions that in the course of the centuries have overlapped and been reciprocally influential. I am, nonetheless, also of the opinion that underneath these institutions we are dealing with two distinct traditions and that the result will be frustrating and confusing until we are as clear about what separates these traditions from each other as we are about the points they have in common.

The Mendicants

I begin with the twelfth century. Although some qualification may be required for monks in their monasteries and priests in cathedral schools, formation for ministry was based on the informal model of apprenticeship within the precincts of a local church. The apprentice learned from his master in a one-on-one situation whatever was required for the fulfillment of his office.

Once the universities were created later in that century, the situation began to change drastically, with developments that over the course of the centuries would eventually become normative. The university formalized and professionalized learning in a measure hitherto unknown through the establishment of set curricula, examinations, and degrees. Formation had moved from the informal one-on-one situation to a rigorous and rather impersonalized corporation.

Moreover, the scholastic, i.e., academic, nature of the learning promoted by the universities meant that it was acquired not through on-the-job training but in the classroom. The universities did not compensate for this change by any programs in what we would call pastoral field education. That same academic quality divorced it from affect—hence, from spirituality. The remote foundations for our current divisions of formation into academic, pastoral, and spiritual find their origins here, even though this change was perceived by only a few contemporaries like Saint Bernard, and only dimly at that.

Although canons regular and a few monks contributed to the creation of the medieval universities, the diocesan clergy were in the earliest days their backbone. As we know well, however, the universities would soon become the location for the training of members of the mendicant orders that were coming into being at about the same time. "Seculars and regulars" lived in an often disharmonious conjunction at the universities, but we do have here one of our first and clearest instances of influences of the former upon the formation of the latter.

The ministry of the early mendicants arose out of a situation that was quite different from the concept of ecclesiastical office characteristic of the diocesan clergy. That ministry was part of the enthusiasm for the *vita apostolica* that swept over western Europe from the twelfth century onward. The image of the "apostolic life" idealized the egalitarianism, the itinerant preaching, and the communal poverty found in Acts and the synoptic gospels. Among the medicants the Franciscans perhaps best embody that ideal, and in some ways it found its most appealing, orthodox, and perfect expression in the life and ministry of Saint Francis. It is to the *Poverello,* therefore, that for a moment I will direct our attention.

Saint Francis based his life and ministry on a radical identification with Jesus as portrayed in the synoptic gospels. This was true to such an extent that in the minds of his followers he was seen as a perfect re-presentation of the life and ministry of Jesus, as we see later exemplified in the widely circulate *Little*

Flowers of Saint Francis. What are some of the constitutive elements in that re-presentation?

Saint Francis was never ordained a priest, did not celebrate Mass or administer the sacraments. His ministry took the form of various ministries of Word. His warrant for this ministry sprang from his inner inspiration, not from office or extrinsic call. He never had a parish, and his radical poverty excluded all other fixed locations for ministry based on benefice. Protected by the hierarchy, he had no other institutional relationship to it. This meant that his ministry would carry him beyond parochial and diocesan lines and eventually lead him outside Christendom itself to preach before the sultan of Egypt.

The ideal embodied by Francis underwent compromise almost immediately, especially as the number of priests recruited into the order grew,[2] but it never surrendered the basic elements of design. Moreover, the ideal would remain a powerfully operative force among both clergy and laity in the Church for centuries to come. We must remember that it was adaptable to both groups and was in fact adopted by both, as the second and third orders and the lay confraternities that sprang up show. Within the order the call of the Franciscan was the call to follow Francis's model of the imitation of Christ, and the contrast that call posed to other models of spirituality and ministry sometimes erupted to the surface, as in the bitter controversies occasioned by the so-called "Spiritual Franciscans" in later centuries.

For all the mendicants the life-time commitment of their call caused them to appropriate certain aspects of the monastic tradition. Their novitiates and convents, modeled on the monasteries, were where that commitment could be further evoked and sustained, so that when the mendicants established themselves in their *studia* at the universities they did so in their convents. In the convents a regimen of discipline and liturgy prevailed that provided for what we might call the ongoing

---

[2]See, e.g., Lawrence C. Landini, *The Cause of the Clericalization of the Order of Friars Minor, 1209-1260, in the Light of Early Franciscan Sources* (Chicago, 1968).

spiritual formation of the friar, providing for him in this regard what the university did not.

The convent model undoubtedly influenced the development of the so-called *collegia* at the universities, which were basically residence halls, even though classes later began to be held in them.[3] The secular clergy living in the colleges soon devised a regimen similar to that of the convents, and by the end of the fifteenth century the discipline in the colleges was often severe, as we know from Erasmus' caustic remarks about the living situation at the College de Montaigu at Paris at that time.[4] Both John Calvin and Ignatius Loyola were later students in that same college.

We need to note several features about the discipline of these colleges, for it would be a silent but important factor in future models of formation. First, the students in the colleges lacked the foundational experience of conversion that the novitiates of the friars supposedly either sustained or evoked. Secondly, the discipline consisted in a routine of rather rudimentary exercises of discipline and piety, like imposed fasts and attendance at Mass and other exercises of devotion. Thirdly, whereas the convents were a continuing feature in the life of the friar even after he left the university, the colleges were temporary situations that little corresponded to the living situation of the diocesan priest in his later life.

We must at this point recall, however, that relatively few diocesan priests attended the university and underwent the discipline of the college. Most future priests continued to live with their families and were still trained in the rather haphazard style of the apprentice, whose efficacy depended almost entirely on the qualities of the master under whom he was formed. Other men found their way almost entirely on their own, especially if they came from the upper strata of society. Philip Neri and Charles Borromeo would be two outstanding examples of this tradition of persons whose theological for-

[3]See, e.g., Gabriel Codina Mir, *Aux sources de la pédagogie des jésuites: Le "modus parisiensis"* (Rome, 1968).

[4]See "Concerning the Eating of Fish" in *The Essential Erasmus*, ed. John P. Dolan (New York, 1964), pp. 320-21.

mation, such as it was, and whose spiritual formation depended almost entirely on their own initiative. As these examples show, the situation was not all bad.

Textbooks sometimes lead us to believe that in 1563 the Council of Trent by its decree on seminaries in the twenty-third session radically changed that situation. That is, of course, not true. Considerable variety in formation would prevail well into the modern era, especially for persons coming from high-placed families. Nonetheless, the tridentine decree was of immense importance both for developments that it actually set under way and for its use as a proof-text for those who, wittingly or unwittingly, would twist its meaning to support ideas the Fathers of the Council never intended.

What, then, did the decree of the Council intend? First of all, it looked towards more effective training for boys from the poorer classes of society and wanted to provide for them that minimum required for basic ritual tasks in the local church, often the parish. The decree nowhere indicates that training in a seminary was to be a necessary prerequisite for ordination for all candidates. Secondly, it placed this opportunity firmly in the hands of the local bishop, thus reaffirming the ancient tradition in this regard, as earlier exemplified by the cathedral school, and similarly underscoring the tridentine preoccupation with shoring up the bishop's pastoral responsibilities in general. Thirdly, it was concerned with providing a safe place for fostering the moral development of the candidate and with providing a training in basic pastoral skills like singing, study of cases of conscience, and the method of performing the rites of the Church. The discipline of theology as it was known in the sixteenth century and as we know it today was given little consideration in this context. No provision whatsoever was made for philosophy. In other words, almost totally missing from the decree is any provision for what we would today term academic formation.

The immediate models for the tridentine decree seem to have been the institutions along similar lines founded about the same time by Gian Matteo Giberti, the reforming bishop of Verona, by Cardinal Reginald Pole in the England of Mary Stuart, and possibly even older institutions in the Iberian peninsula.[5] Although the decree uses the word seminary to describe what it means, the term most frequently used is college, thereby suggesting that the more remote model was the university institution I earlier described. The great difference from that institution in the tridentine use of the term is that the college the Council envisions stands free—without any university affiliation.

The Jesuits and Trent

By 1563, however, other models had sprung into existence and were well known to those who framed the decree. Most important among them were certain institutions founded by the nascent Society of Jesus, particularly the *Collegium Germanicum,* established in Rome by the Jesuits in 1552.[6] The principal patron of the *Germanicum* was Giovanni Cardinal Morone, chief papal legate to the Council in 1562-63, the so-called "savior of the Council of Trent." In general terms the tridentine decree takes account of this and similar institutions and tries indirectly to help their financing.

We must keep in mind that the Jesuits who found the *Germanicum* were graduates of the University of Paris and had lived in its colleges. Recent research is unanimous in its affirmation of the impact that the *modus parisiensis*—the Parisian style of education—had on all the Jesuits' educational endeavors.[7] The Jesuits' premier institution was the Roman College, which almost immediately took on most of the features of a medieval university in its establishment of faculties of philosophy and theology as well as the so-called lower faculty of the humanities. That last faculty reflected the

---

[5]See, e.g., James A. O'Donohoe, "The Seminary Legislation of the Council of Trent," in *II Concilio di Trento e la riforma tridentina,* 2 vols. (Rome, 1965), 157-72.

[6]See Peter Schmidt, *Das Collegium Germanicum in Rom und die Germaniker: Zur Funktion eines römischen Ausländerseminars, 1552-1914* (Tübingen, 1984).

[7]See Codina Mir, *Aux sources.*

attempts of the University of Paris to take account of some of
the features of the new literary education that we know as
Renaissance Humanism. It was that faculty that appealed most
directly to students who were not pursuing a clerical career,
but in elite circles the worldly learning it represented was
already considered indispensable for the well-trained cleric as
well. Jesuits studied at the Roman College, but from the
beginning it was open to all qualified students. In fact, by the
time Saint Ignatius died in 1556 there was not a single institution in the Society of Jesus in which Jesuits studied apart
from lay students.

Hardly had the Roman College opened its doors when
plans were under way to found a subsidiary college for
candidates for ordination from the German Empire. From the
beginning, the discipline of that college resembled the discipline
of the colleges at Paris. There were, however, some differences.
In many ways the discipline was mitigated. Moreover, some
Jesuits lived in the college and were in general charge of its
regimen. Finally, by insisting that the students before or shortly
after their entrance make at least the First Week of the
Spiritual Exercises, the Jesuits tried to replicate features that
were found most effective in the spiritual formation of their
own members, and they consistently showed reluctance to be
satisfied with merely the observance of an external code.
Although founded for clerics, almost from the beginning lay
students who attended the Roman College also lodged in the
Germanicum. Perhaps the most salient feature of the *Germanicum,* however, was that, while its students resided in the
college, they followed the full course of studies of the
humanities, philosophy, and theology at the Roman College.

As is well known, other colleges were later founded in Rome
on the model of the *Germanicum,* but we should not think of
the Roman situation as an exception to the general rule of
what happened after Trent. Somewhat similar patterns came
into being at Douai, Louvain, Salamanca and elsewhere. At
the Jesuit university at Pont-á-Mousson in France in 1617,
whose almost two thousand students were primarily laymen,
for instance, forty-four Jesuit scholastics were in studies.
Attached to the university as well were three seminaries with

students from three different dioceses, as well as several convents of students from other religious orders.[8]

What we see in these examples are some of the first direct interactions of religious models of formation on the diocesan clergy. We must pause for a moment to recognize that under the surface there were some unresolved discrepancies in the ideals that motivated the Jesuits and the diocesan candidates in their charge. As I read the early Jesuit documents, I am struck, for instance, at the central place that the idea of vocation plays in them. Surely derived from Saint Thomas and other theologians of the mendicant orders is the conviction that vocation is an inner call, an inner call to the order as founded by Saint Ignatius, an inner call shared by the priests of the order and its many laymen—scholastics and brothers. Nowhere does one read of a call to the priesthood as such.

Similarly striking is the fact that the ministries of the order, except for the hearing of confessions and the administration of the Eucharist, are performed rather indiscriminately by scholastics and priests alike. The so-called "Autobiography" importuned from Ignatius shortly before his death was intended to be and was in fact widely utilized within the order as the model for life and ministry of the Jesuit—that document relates his life only up to his ordination. In an important document addressed to Charles Borromeo in 1572, Jerónimo Nadal, Ignatius' best interpreter, insists that even the novices are trained in the ministries of the order and that as novices they begin to exercise them.[9]

The other documents of the order clearly distinguish between the fixed cure of souls proper to the diocesan clergy and the ministries of the Society, which are primarily intended for those who for one reason or another fall outside those limits. The intense labors of the early Jesuits with prostitutes, orphans, prisoners in jail, heretics, and especially their schools and their evangelization of infidels in distant lands most graphically

---

[8]See Joseph M. O'Keefe, "The Pedagogy of Persuasion: Jesuit Education at Pont-a-Mousson," STL thesis, Weston School of Theology, Cambridge, MA, 1989.

[9]"Tractatus de professione et choro," in *Monumenta Nadal* IV (Monumenta Historica Societatis Jesu), 165-81.

illustrate what is intended. I myself am not altogether convinced that the program of training the Jesuits devised for their members perfectly correlated with the ministries they envisioned for them, but I believe it is clear that those ministries and the considerations that underlay them were in any case clearly understood to be different in principle from what was proper to diocesan priests and required training in different skills.

What was happening, meanwhile, to the diocesan seminary legislated by Trent? As we might expect, it has a very uneven history well into the seventeenth century, if not beyond. Immediately after the Council several important seminaries were founded, especially those that were directly or indirectly inspired by Charles Borromeo in his archdiocese and province. Saint Charles forbade the Jesuit teachers in his own seminary to use the pagan classics in their instruction, which suggests to me his well attested model of a clergy with a different culture and spirituality than the laity.[10] Saint Charles did show, however, particular interest in the new forms of preaching that were being devised partly under the influence of the Humanist movement, and he insisted on them as part of the pastoral training in his seminary.

Saint Charles seems to have been the first bishop to instate the retreat as an integral part of the spiritual formation of the seminarian. He required of them an annual retreat of eight days and a month of special spiritual preparation before ordination to the subdiaconate and priesthood. His example was followed by other bishops, as we know from the clear records of the dioceses of Aix and Siena. In the seventeenth century in Paris Saint Vincent de Paul conducted retreats of ten days for the ordinands of the diocese of Paris, and the institution was well on its way towards codification. In other words, the external discipline of the seminary was no longer considered the adequate preparation for ordination to ministry.

The diocese of Novara, under the leadership of Carlo

---

[10]See Mario Scaduto, "Scuola e cultura a Milano nell'età borromaica" in *San Carlo e il suo tempo: Atti del convegno internazionale nel IV cenenario della morte* (Rome, 1986), pp. 963-94.

Bascapè, a disciple of Borromeo, pursued a vigorous policy, and by 1593 had three seminaries—but with a total enrollment of only thirty-three students.[11] Bascapè's policy was intelligent, but like Borromeo himself and most other bishops, he made no provision for theology other than cases of conscience. There was no training in scriptural exegesis.

Even in the Roman Seminary, founded in 1564 and put immediately under the supervision of the Jesuits, only a few of the clerical students attended classes in theology at the Roman College to which it was attached. Saint Robert Bellarmine objected to this policy before he died in 1621, but to no effect. At that seminary, however, within two years after its founding no less a person than Giovanni Pierluigi Palestrina was hired as *Maestro di Capella,* despite the Jesuits' caution regarding training in chant and liturgical music for their own members. The hiring of Palestrina indiates the high calibre of professional training in at least one aspect of what we might call pastoral formation. It is also interesting to note that within a few years after the founding of the *Seminario Romano* the number of lay students in residence there began to surpass the number of young clerics. In 1639, for instance, there were 130 of the former and only forty of the latter.[12]

Despite the great reforming impulses that animated the Spanish church during this period, the seminary had a checkered history, and it is clear that at least well into the eighteenth century bypassing the seminary led to greater preferment if the priest had attended a university. As a recent study states, the cathedral canons who generally directed the Spanish seminaries regarded their students as not much more than sources of free labor to arrange chairs, pump organs, and otherwise assist in the liturgical services of the cathedral.[13]

[11]See Thomas Deutscher, "Seminaries and the Education of Novarese Parish Priests, 1593-1627," *Journal of Ecclesiastical History,* 32 (1981), 303-19.

[12]See Ricardo García Villoslada, "Algunos dócumentos sobre la música en el antiguo seminario romano," *Archivum Historicum Societatis Jesu,* 31 (1962), 107-38.

[13]See Wiliam J. Callahan, *Church, Politics, and Society in Spain, 1750-1874* (Cambridge, MA, 1984), quoted in Grendler, "Schools, Seminaries," p. 324.

Because of its disturbed political situation, France lagged notably behind even Spain in establishing seminaries. It was not until 1696, close to a century and a half after the close of Trent, that a diocesan seminary was established in Paris and attendance made compulsory for ordination. Only by the following century did most French dioceses finally have their local seminary, where training lasted for a few months or several years, depending on the resources and wishes of the bishop. The most notable development in France occurred earlier, however, through the labors of Vincent de Paul and Jean-Jacques Olier, founder of the seminary of Saint-Sulpice in 1642. At Saint Sulpice candidates took their courses at the university, but within the seminary they were given a spiritual training, again of undetermined length according to the discretion of their bishop.

Of crucial importance, of course, was the elaboration in France in the seventeenth century of a spirituality specifically for diocesan priests based on the model of the risen Christ as priest and victim, an ideal that would be elaborated upon and extended to priests in religious orders in a virtual flood of pious literature up to our own days.[14] Concomitant with this development was the articulation of the idea of vocation to the priesthood as an inner call, similar to the call to religious life that had been taken up and elaborated upon for centuries by the mendicants and their successors. This idea long competed with the idea that the vocation to diocesan priesthood consisted rather in the external call to service issued by the candidate's prelate, which was solemnly reaffirmed as the traditional interpretation of vocation by a commission of cardinals as late as 1912. Soon thereafter, however, the other idea of priestly vocation began clearly to prevail and won the day.[15]

The Period after Vatican II

I will here draw this sketchy and panoramic review to a close. Two historical pieces by Joseph White and myself appear

---

[14]See, e.g., Eugene Walsh, *The Priesthood in the Writings of the French School: Berulle, de Condren, Olier* (Washington, 1949).

[15]See the article on "vocation" in *Dictionnaire de théologie catholique,* especially cols. 3171-74.

in the study by Katarina Schuth, *Reason for the Hope.* I also call your attention to the new book by Christopher J. Kauffman on the Sulpicians in the United States.[16] These two studies are especially valuable sources for what happened in our own country in the nineteenth and twentieth centuries. If I had to summarize in a few words what happened, I would say that until Vatican II candidates for ordination for both dioceses and religious orders began to be trained in institutions that were ever more remote from centers of learning and culture (despite some eloquent objections to this development). These institutions came to be considered the only path to ordination open to these candidates, they admitted no students except candidates for ordination, they came increasingly to be regulated by decrees emanating from Roman Congregations, and, consequently, they became ever more standardized in their programs of both academic and spiritual formation—"one size fits all."

Let me now turn to the documents of Vatican II that are pertinent to our topic—the decrees on religious life, on the office of bishop, on the life and ministry of priests, and on the training of priests. I will here be brief because I have published my thoughts on this matter in a long article in the June number of *Theological Studies* last year.[17] The point of my article was simply that these documents, as well as subsequent ones inspired by them, do not take adequate account of the religious clergy and rest on the silent assumption that the model for them is basically the same as that for their brothers in the diocesan clergy.

From the historical developments I have outlined it is easy to see the basis grounding this assumption. When one looks simply at the history of the institutions of formation for ministry, one is impressed by the sometimes parallel, sometimes overlapping developments and by the almost constant reciprocity of influence. When one looks at other factors, however,

---

[16] *Tradition and Transformation in Catholic Culture: The Priests of Saint Sulpice in the United States from 1791 to the Present* (New York, 1988).

[17] "Priesthood, Ministry, and Religious Life: Some Historical and Historiographical Considerations," *Theological Studies,* 49 (1988), 223-57.

the picture that emerges is far less univocal.

The basic design undergirding the document of the Council on the episcopacy and the two on priests rests, in my opinion, on three essential components: (1) priestly ministry is by and large conceived as ministry to the faithful; (2) it is ministry done, therefore, within the community of faith that is the parish and ministry intimately related to the office of pastor; (3) it is ministry done "in hierarchical union with the order of bishops." The design corresponds to the traditions and ministry of the diocesan clergy as we have known it in history and in the present. Does it correspond to the traditions of the regular clergy? Not so clearly! In fact, in some ways it almost contradicts them.

The decree on religious life, where one might expect to find a balancing of considerations, rests on the framework of the pursuit of personal perfection through religious discipline and the three vows. Of the twenty-five sections of the document, only two relate to ministry, despite the fact that since the thirteenth century most orders of men were founded for ministry and since the seventeenth most orders of women. One has the impression that ministry is an ornament added to the excellence of religious life, not its very constitution. From this source, therefore, we derive little help in rectifying the perspective of the other documents.

I do not wish to seem to be harsh on the Council. As I point out at length in my article, the Council made the best use it could of the insights and scholarship that was available to it. What I try to show, rather, is that we have been heirs to historiographical traditions that are lopsided and inadequate to the realities they tried to describe. This was true of religious, who consistently wrote of their vocation in terms of what I call "the Pachomius to Ignatius" tradition, i.e., religious life was simply an unfolding and elaboration of the cenobitic tradition of asceticism and spirituality. Little attention was given to the implications of different ministries and styles of ministry. The result was that the religious clergy were left somewhat confounded by the documents of the Council.

I think I illustrate this reality from the recent history of the Society of Jesus. As best I know, the first time in the history of the Society that the subject of *priestly* ministry was officially considered was in a brief document issued by the Thirty-First Congregation of the Society that met just as Vatican II ended.[18] That document was obviously meant to be a positive response to the correlative documents of the Council, but it flipflops uncertainly this way and that in trying to come to terms with them.

That Congregation and the two that have met since then found themselves much more at ease with the documents of the Council on ecumenism, evangelization, and "the Church in the modern world." I think that fact is significant. I cannot speak for members of other orders or congregations, but I suspect the same would be true for many of them. In any case, these documents do not look to parish, to liturgical ministry, or in some cases to ministry primarily to the faithful, and they at least suggest that preparation to deal effectively with the realities treated in them must be somewhat different from preparation to deal more exclusively with women and men in the pews. Let me put the matter in the form of a blunt question: In today's Church should the same model of spiritual, pastoral, and academic preparation for ministry be imposed on both the diocesan and religious clergy?

With that question I have obviously concluded the first two parts of my presentation and am leading into some reflections I would propose for your consideration.

1. I think that in the past, while there has often been a distinction of institutions in which the diocesan and religious clergy have been trained, for various reasons these institutions have not always adequately reflected the distinction of ministries for which candidates were intended. We may be in a better position to do this than were previous generations, although one obstacle to accomplishing this goal is the passion for homogenization abroad in the world that is having its impact on the Church. Another obstacle is a lack of clarity, aside from the primacy of parish liturgy for the diocesan

---

[18]"The Jesuit Priestly Apostolate" in *Documents of the 31st and 32nd General Congregations of the Society of Jesus* (St. Louis, 1977), pp. 199-205.

priests, regarding what those ministries are and how they are to be exercised. But the basic question about formation remains: does one size fit all?

2. Despite a lot of similarity among institutions in which religious and diocesan candidates for priesthood have been trained, I believe I detect beneath the surface some important but unresolved issues about the nature of vocation to ministry, especially among religious. Is one called primarily to be a Franciscan, or is one called primarily to be a priest? Have we, moreover, adequately explored regarding religious priests the relationship of the vows to ministry and ordination?

3. This raises the question of priestly spirituality. The very term suggests a spirituality that is proper to priests almost as a class, one might say. The idea of such a spirituality began to taken on clear contours in the seventeenth century, and achieved widespread articulation in the years just before Vatican II. Yet the spirituality of the religious orders has been by definition available to anybody who desired to follow it— man or woman, lay person or cleric. Have we not been too facile in our synthesis in this regard, which results today in a sense that the issue requires more scrutiny than we have given it?

4. Christ, of course, is the basic model for Christian ministry, but to which "portrait of Jesus" does one look? Is it "Christ the priest" or Jesus the itinerant preacher in search of the lost sheep? More proximately, does not Francis the layman (later deacon) embody an ideal different from that of Jean-Baptiste Vianney, parish priest at Ars? What do we make of discrepancies like these?

5. The above issue is an issue of relationships. Let me, then, raise another. Just how is it that religious priests operate "in hierarchical union with the order of bishops," as Vatican II says?

6. Let me conclude by raising an issue that struck me during a recent symposium I attended on spiritual formation for ministry at which I was one of the few Catholic participants. The big difference between the Catholic and the other models was the immense apparatus Catholics have assembled for spiritual formation, as contrasted with Protestant emphasis on

all formation as being done primarily in the classroom. The Protestants were eager to learn from the Catholics, but I wonder if we Catholics do not still have a great deal to accomplish in overcoming the compartmentalization into academic, pastoral and spiritual formation that we find exemplified in both the diocesan and religious traditions from the thirteenth century forward.[19]

[19]The papers of the symposium will be published shortly by The Center on Religion and Society. My contribution is entitled: "Spiritual Formation for Ministry: Some Roman Catholic Traditions—Their Past and Present."

The Priesthood of Jesus Christ in the Ministry and Life of the Ordained

Peter E. Fink, S.J.

The reflections that follow represent a systematic attempt to understand a single affirmation of the church's magisterium, namely, that the priesthood of the ordained differs from the priesthood of the baptized "essentially and not only in degree."[1] The complementary question of relationship and difference among the three orders will be there in the background, and occasionally in the foreground, but this is not the issue of primary concern.[2]

The attempt is made for two reasons. The first is the theological task itself, whereby faith always seeks to be understood (*fides quaerens intellectum*). The second is a pastoral

---

[1] *Lumen Gentium* (henceforth, LG), II, 10. This affirmation of the Church's faith has a long and noble history, which, however, is not the subject of this paper. For the purpose of these reflections, its reaffirmation in LG is taken as point of departure. In addition to LG, two other major sources will be tapped: *Sacrosanctum Concilium* (SC) on the Sacred Liturgy, and the revised rites of ordination promulgated by Paul VI, June 16, 1968.

[2] The question of both difference and relationship among the three orders of bishop, presbyter and deacon requires that two things be taken into account. On the one hand, there is the language of distinction: bishop possesses fullness of priesthood, the presbyteral order is a distinct rank of priesthood, the deacon is ordained "not unto priesthood, but to service" (LG, III, 29). On the other hand, there is the unity of the sacrament of orders specified by the common gesture of the laying on of hands and the consecration prayer that invokes the Spirit upon the ordained. Deacon, presbyter and bishop are unequivocally named recipients of the sacrament of orders. In this paper the unity of the sacrament of orders is considered primary, the distinctions to be assessed within that unity.

concern, to deepen a sense of identity and purpose in those who are going to be, or who are already, ordained to ministry in the church.

A Contemporary Challenge

There are some who call into question the essential difference between the priesthood of the ordained and that of the baptized. In part, this is due to the relatively recent recovery in Roman Catholic circles of the concept "priesthood of the faithful," and to the priority given to the laity in the wake of Vatican II. There is thus the inevitable tendency upon such recovery to exaggerate what had been neglected and play down what had been given prominence. It is also due, in part, to the tendency among many to reduce ordained ministry to function, and to view ordination as anything from recognition of gifts to simple appointment. The question, "why do you have to be ordained to preach?" is but one instance of this kind of reduction. There are no doubt other factors as well, but these two seem the most cogent.

There is also, as recent study by the US-American bishops has noted, a problem of morale among those who are ordained, which cannot help but influence those advancing to orders as well. Two things, among no doubt many more, contribute to this: the failure of traditional language to speak convincingly of the significance of ordained priesthood as a distinct and important ministry in the church and the emergence of a variety of lay ministers who are in fact doing what was once the preserve of ordained priests.[3] Priests cannot help but wonder "what's left," and if it is any more what they once gave their lives for? People advancing to priesthood cannot help but ask if it is in fact worth giving a life for?

The theological task and the pastoral purpose set for these reflections are thus timely and well placed.

---

[3]The issue of celibacy contributes to this as well, but it is beyond the scope and intent of this paper to address this.

Clarifying the Terms

A first step in approaching the question is to clarify the terms of the assertion. Three terms in particular need attention. The priesthood of the ordained is said to *differ* from that of the baptized, not only in *degree,* but also in *essence.* Clarification of these three terms will already take us well into the pursuit before us.

(a) *Difference.* The first thing that needs to be determined is how the term "differ" is used in this assertion. Difference is frequently determined by exclusive definition, that is, by setting one reality apart from, and even over against, another. It is true the oft-cited text from Hebrews, which has been appropriated in Catholic tradition for the ordained priesthood, speaks of priests being "chosen from among" the people, and that *Lumen Gentium* defines clergy and laity as exclusive of each other (LG, IV, 31).[4] Nonetheless, where the term "priesthood" is applied to both the baptized and the ordained, it is not used in a strictly exclusive way.

The full text from *Lumen Gentium,* already cited in part above, reads: "Though they differ essentially and not only in degree, the common priesthood of the faithful and the ministerial or hierarchical priesthood are nonetheless ordered one to another; each in its own proper way shares in the one priesthood of Christ" (LG, II, 10). There is a fundamental relationship between the two that is rooted in the one priesthood of Jesus Christ. Moreover, each is properly understood only as ordered to the other, that is in light of that fundamental relationship. Where distinctions are drawn between the two, it is only in terms of specific and proper ways in which each shares in Christ's priesthood. Differences that are named must be understood in light of this relationship, rather than exclusively, or over against each other.

An analogy may be drawn to the difference between

---

[4]It also defines religious as a third category, neither clergy nor lay. The significance of this definition, also beyond the scope of this paper, would need to be assessed in a full treatment of the ways in which the priesthood of Christ is made manifest in the church.

husband and wife in marriage. Before marriage, and apart from the relationship which marriage establishes and consecrates, a man and a woman may be defined exclusively. The man is other than the woman; the woman, other than the man. Within marriage, however, husband and wife can only be defined relationally. Husband is husband *to* wife; wife is wife *to* husband. The identity of each is established within a more fundamental union between them. Moreover, in that relationship each is constitutive of the other. Husband constitutes wife as wife; wife constitutes husband as husband. The fundamental unity of "two in one flesh" constitutes each to be who they are in relationship.

If the analogy holds, and if the relationship between the priesthood of the ordained and the priesthood of the baptized is recognized to be a mutual relationship, each ordered "one to another," as LG asserts, it is possible to say that priesthood of the ordained is priesthood *to* the priesthood of the baptized and that priesthood of the baptized is priesthood *to* the priesthood of the ordained. It is possible to say, moreover, that each constitutes the other as a distinct mode of Christ's priesthood: ordained priesthood of the baptized constitutes priesthood of the ordained. And the fundamental unity of the priesthood of Christ, made manifest in different ways in each, constitutes the priesthood of both.

The terms of this mutuality are yet to be determined. It is important at this point only to recognize that the way the term "differ" operates in this assertion of the church's faith is as a difference in relationship, and not a difference of exclusion.

(b) *Degree.* The term "degree" must also be carefully examined. Its usual connotation is of quantitative gradation, read on such scales as higher or lower, fuller or less full, more important or less important. Some of the language within the sacrament of orders reflects this kind of gradation, as, for example, advancing in rank or promotion to a higher order. In addition, the language used for bishop, as possessing "the fullness of the priesthood," is suggestive of the same, implying at least that such fullness is not present elsewhere.

Nonetheless, this kind of quantitative gradation is misleading and finally not helpful. It is not helpful among the three orders, and it is not helpful to distinguish priesthood of the ordained from that of the faithful. While the bishop is indeed said to possess the fullness of the priesthood, nowhere is it said explicitly that presbyter or deacon possess it only partially. On the contrary, the presbyter is named "co-worker" of the bishop and "sharer" in his priesthood, that is, sharer in the fullness of the priesthood of Christ. And in spite of the disclaimer that the "deacon is not ordained unto priesthood, but to service," the deacon too is named "helper" of the bishop and his body of priests. The deacon too, at the discretion of the bishop, may be authorized to perform ministries that are proper to the bishop himself, that is, proper to the fullness of priesthood.[5]

What is called the fullness of priesthood is constituted by the triple ministry of prophet, priest and pastor, that is, proclaiming the Word, offering of gifts, governing the people. This triple ministry is listed for bishop, certainly. Yet it is also listed for presbyter, for deacon, and indeed for the laity as well.[6]

The priesthood of Christ is not a quantity to be doled out in portions. It is a mystery to be shared in different ways and to be participated in to different degrees. This language of "sharing in" and "participating in" is very different from

[5]It is not clear why a line is drawn between the presbyterate and the diaconate, especially in light of the unity of the sacrament of orders. Popular language that considers permanent deacons as "lay deacons" is clearly inappropriate. Oddly enough, the quote cited here in regard to deacons is only a partial quote. The full text reads: "deacon is not ordained to priesthood but to service *of the bishop.*" The deacon is far more linked to the office and ministry of the bishop, and therefore to the fullness of priesthood, than the text usually cited implies.

[6]This is clear for presbyters who are said to "consitute one priesthood with their bishop" (LG, III, 28), and who are asked to proclaim the word, offer the gifts of the people, and to share with the bishop in the work of Christ, the Head and Shepherd of the Church. It is equally clear for the laity, who "in their own way share the priestly, prophetic and kingly office of Christ" (LG, IV, 31), and whom Christ intimately associates with his life and mission, to whom he gives "a share in His priestly function of offering spiritual worship for the glory of God" (LG, IV, 34). It is perhaps less clear for the deacon, who remains somewhat of an anomaly. Yet deacons are assigned the ministry of proclamation, are asked to "preside at the worship and prayer of the faithful" (Instruction of Ordination rite), and are dedicated to "duties of charity and administration" (LG, III, 29) which surely involve them in the pastoral office of the bishop.

language that suggests full or partial possession. It must be said that only Jesus Christ possesses the fullness of his priesthood, and that the primary manifestation of the priesthood of Christ is the church in its entirety.[7] Different modes of participation, and different degrees of participation, must be understood within this sacramental identity of the whole church with the mystery of Christ.

How then to understand the difference in degree between the priesthood of the faithful and the priesthood of the ordained? What is in fact being measured here? A clue can be gotten from the reason for which the apostolic office is established. It is established for pastoral care of the church (LG, I, 8). A second clue can be gotten by focusing in on that particular pastoral care which is embraced by the term priesthood: proclamation of the word, offering of gifts, pastoral governance and guidance of the church. The pastoral care involved in priesthood is specific, not generic. A final clue can be gotten by calling forth one-half of the mutual relationship between the two modes of Christ's priesthood mentioned above, namely, that ordained priesthood exists *for* and is *ordered to* the priesthood of the faithful.

The ordained minister preaches in order to awaken the summons of the word in others. He prays and offers in order to awaken prayer and offering in others. He guides and governs in order to awaken and shape in others that same pastoral care to each other that Christ shows to all. In other words, ordained ministers exercise the priesthood of the ordained in order to awaken in the baptized their own proper priesthood. But this is more than simple task or function. It is a ministry that demands of the minister an entrance into and a conformity with the mystery of Christ's own priesthood that is and must be more invested and more intense than it is for those who are being ministered to. Put simply, it demands more of the person to preach than to listen, to lead prayer than be led in prayer, to govern and guide than be governed and guided.

The ordination rites in fact recognize this. The deacon is

---

[7]See, SC, 2 where the nature of the church and the mystery of Christ are identified.

required, as an essential part of the ministry assigned him, to "believe what you read, preach what you believe, and put into practice what you preach" (Ordination rite, at commissioning of the Gospel). The presbyter is required, as an essential part of the ministry assigned him, to "know what you are doing and imitate the mystery you celebrate" (Ordination rite, Instruction). And the bishop is required, as an essential part of the ministry assigned him, to embody the counsel and example of the Master: "the greater should behave as if he were the least, and the leader as if he were the one who serves," and to be mindful of the Good Shepherd, "who knows his sheep and is known by them and who did not hesitate to lay down his life for them" (Ordination rite, Instruction).

These are more than pious admonitions. They are solemn commissions by the church to bishop, presbyter and deacon to enter into the mystery of Christ's own priesthood more profoundly, and with greater personal investment than others, for the sake of the others who will thus be served. The difference of degree can be located right here. Degree of closeness, degree of intensity, degree of personal investment in the Word, the sacrifice, and the pastoral care of Jesus Christ himself. It is not a quantitative measure that gives power or prestige. It is rather one which names the mission and the ministry which the church asks of those who are ordained and specifies the personal cost of that mission and ministry.

(c) *Essence.* The most crucial term, difference in *kind* or *essence,* can only properly be understood if the relationship between the two modes of priesthood and their unity in the one priesthood of Christ is rigorously maintained. The key to the difference is that each, *in its own proper way,* manifests the priesthood of Christ. They are not two different priesthoods, differing one from the other as do apples and oranges. They are two different manifestations of one and the same priesthood which belongs to Christ and to Christ alone.

A static notion of essence or kind does not serve the faith of the church at this point. Statically understood, essence is indistinguishable from entity, and if the priesthood of the ordained and the priesthood of the baptized are viewed as two different entities, their participation in the priesthood of Christ, which would have to be considered a third entity, could only be extrinsic. Delicate language such as the affirmation that the priest stands *in persona Christi* or that the church assembled is a *sacramentum Christi* could yield only language of substitution, that is, the priest *in place of* Christ or the church *in place of* Christ, or, within the sacrament of orders itself, the presbyter *in place of* the bishop. While this language is in fact sometimes employed, it does present a severely restricted, and inaccurate, view of the sacramental nature of the church as a whole and of ordained ministry within the church. Christ is not absent from the church and its ministry. Christ is present at its very depth. No human reality substitutes for Christ. Sacramental human realities make Christ present.

The term essence here needs to be recaptured as a dynamic reality. It is, as LG makes clear, a mode of sharing or a mode of participating in Christ's priesthood, and this sharing is intrinsic, not extrinsic. The language of SC is helpful here, that the mystery of Christ is *brought to expression* (SC, 2). *Sacramentum Christi* brings the mystery of Christ to visible and tangible expression. One who serves *in persona Christi* brings the mystery of Christ to visible and tangible expression. Something of inner depth is unveiled. The unity of the one priesthood of Christ is preserved.

Seen in light of the more fundamental relationship between the priesthood of Christ made manifest in and expressed in the ordained and the priesthood of Christ made manifest in and expressed in the baptized, this dynamism includes within itself the ordering to the other which LG affirms of each. It includes, moreover, the power to call forth something in the other. The priesthood of Christ made manifest in the ordained *is* the dynamism that awakens the priesthood of Christ in the baptized. Conversely, the priesthood of Christ made manifest in the baptized *is* the dynamism that summons forth priesthood in the ordained.[8] Each is essentially different from the other

---

[8] It is a common observation among ordained priests that they come to know their priesthood when and as it is called forth by those whom they serve. It is no less true, if less commonly observed, that the faithful will know the priesthood that is theirs only when and as it is called forth by the ministry of the ordained.

because each is ordered to and dependent on the other.

It is part of the mystery of Christ's own priesthood that it could not activate itself; it had to be drawn out by Another, Abba. "Christ became obedient unto death" (Phil 2:8). That truth of Christ's priesthood continues to hold as it comes to expression in the church. It cannot exist in one form alone. The priesthood of Christ requires two different modes of expression precisely because of its deepest truth, that it cannot be activated from within itself, but must be called forth from another.

It is in this mutual ordering to the other that the "essential" difference between priesthood of the ordained and the common priesthood of the faithful is to be found. Just as husband, who calls forth wife to be wife, is essentially different from wife, who calls forth husband to be husband, where the essential difference consists precisely in being directed to the other, so the dynamism of priesthood is essentially different in each because in each it is ordered and directed to the other.

The Presence of Christ

Clarification of terms does serve as a first step in understanding the affirmation of the church's magisterium which is under investigation, that the priesthood of the ordained differs essentially and not merely in degree from the common priesthood of the faithful. Both appear as manifestations of the priesthood of Christ, or better, as manifestations of Christ our priest. Since, indeed, we are dealing here with two different manifestations of the presence of Christ, the advance made by Vatican II on this eucharistic question can take us to another level of understanding of our own.

The question of eucharistic presence has for centuries been limited in focus to the consecrated bread and wine. Vatican II expanded the question to include three other modes of Christ's presence: the Word, the priest or minister, and the assembly itself (SC, 7). What makes this expansion pertinent to our own question here is that SC immediately draws this four-fold presence of Christ into the question of Christ's priesthood.

> Christ, indeed, always associates the church with himself in this great work in which God is perfectly glorified and men are sanctified.... The liturgy, then, is rightly seen as an exercise of the priestly office of Jesus Christ. It involves the presentation of man's sanctification under the guise of signs perceptible by the senses and its accomplishment in ways appropriate to each of these signs. In it full public worship is performed by the Mystical Body of Jesus Christ, that is, by the Head and his members (SC, 7).

The presence of Christ and the priesthood of Christ are inseparable.

The presence of Christ in the eucharist is a single presence, brought forth to expression in four distinct modes. Pre-eminence continues to be given to his presence in the eucharistic food, but this in no way negates the reality of Christ's presence in the other three. "This presence of Christ under the species is called *real* not in any exclusive sense, as if the other kinds of presence were not real, but *par excellence.*"[9] Since two of the modes of Christ's real presence are the assembly and the presiding priest/ minister, understanding of the distinction here cannot help but illuminate the distinction between priesthood of the ordained and common priesthood of the faithful.

Walter Brueggemann has pointed out that the Jewish experience of God found expression in four distinct sets of symbols, and that this same four-fold set of symbols was appropriated by early Christians to capture and name their experience of the presence of Christ.[10] For Jews, God was experienced as one who *comes, leads, abides* and *hides.* For Christians, Christ was experienced as one who *comes, leads, abides* and *hides.* And each of these experiences is radically different. One who comes surprises us. One who leads draws something out of us, takes us somewhere. One who abides

[9] 1967 Instruction on Eucharistic Worship, 9.

[10] See, W. Brueggemann, "The Presence of God," in *The Interpreter's Dictionary of the Bible,* Supplementary Volume (Nashville: Abingdon, 1976), 680-683. See also my "Perceiving the Presence of Christ," in *Worship* 58 (Jan 84), 17-28.

assures us. And one who hides needs to be called forth or unveiled.

A correspondence can be drawn between these four sets of symbols required to bring forth and express the presence of Christ and the four modes of Christ's presence in the eucharist. In Word Christ *comes*. In presiding priest/minister Christ *leads*. In eucharistic food Christ *abides*. And in assembly Christ *hides*. Each of these represents a different way in which Christ's presence is experienced.

On one level, we can single out the second and the fourth as naming the priesthood of the ordained and the priesthood of the baptized. In the baptized the priesthood of Christ lies hidden, needing to be identified, needing to be called forth. In the ordained, the priesthood of Christ leads, goes before, and serves to call forth what is hidden. In the re-organization of the liturgical books, the *Sacramentary*, which is the presider's book, identifies the two primary ministries of ordained presider: to call into unity the assembly of Christ and to lead that assembly in the prayer of Christ. This is the purpose for which Christ is present under this particular mode of *leadership*. It names with even greater specificity what was already set forth above, that the priesthood of the ordained exists to call forth the baptized into their own proper priesthood.

On another level, there is a correspondence between two of the four modes and the triple ministry of Christ's priesthood, namely, proclamation of Word (prophet), presider-leader of prayer (priest) and presider-summoner of the assembly (pastor). The fourth, the assembly, both asks that these ministries be done, and thus calls them forth, and receives these ministries as an awakening in themselves of what lies hidden. The third, the sign of the *abiding* presence, not only serves to assure the church of Christ's on-going and permanent presence in the church, but identifies why ordination itself is enacted on ministers of Word, of offering, and of governance. It is precisely to speak that assurance upon those ministers and their ministries, both for themselves and for those who will be ministered to. It is precisely to assure that in the mutual interaction between ordained and baptized it is the one Christ present who operates from within each to awaken priesthood in both.

The word *consecration* names that assurance in eucharistic food. The food is transformed into the presence of Christ; Christ is truly present in the food that is transformed. This same word, this same act, lies at the heart of ordination. The minister of Word, of offering, of governance is transformed into the presence of Christ; Christ is truly present in the persons who are transformed. And all this is to ensure and guarantee the transformation of the church as a whole as the church hears the word, is summoned into Christ's own prayer, and is formed in communion by Christ himself.

This brief reflection on the four-fold presence of Christ in the eucharist sheds further light on the identity and mission of the ordained deacon, presbyter and bishop and on the triple ministry of Christ's priesthood which is proper to the bishop and shared in specific ways by both presbyters and deacons. Each is consecrated to be a *sacramentum Christi* in the deepest sense of the word—not to substitute for Christ, but to serve Christ who is present and who reaches out from within their own human person and ministry to touch and transform the people of the church. In the laying on of hands and its accompanying prayer of consecration, Christ's Spirit is invoked upon them and called out from within them. Christ is thus made present in them as one to be trusted henceforth by both the people of the church and the ministers themselves as the deepest truth of the otherwise all too human ministry that they provide. Theology will speak of *character* impressed upon the person ordained. It is nothing less than the guarantee of faith that human ministry carries and unveils Christ's own ministry to us all.

The Normative Eucharist

Reflection on the four-fold presence of Christ in the eucharist not only illuminates further the distinction-in-relation between the priesthood of the ordained and the priesthood of the baptized. It also sheds light on the significance of ordination in the life of the church. Ordination assures the transformation and consecration that the ministry given to the ordained requires. Ordination is, after all, the act by which ordained bishops, presbyters, and deacons are established in and for the church. It must inevitably be included in any reflection that seeks to understand the ministry and life of the ordained.

Some further reflection on the act of ordination can unveil yet another truth of the priesthood of the ordained. Ordination is a liturgical act of the church. As such, it is a solemn action of "the Mystical Body of Jesus Christ, that is, by the Head and its members" (SC, 7). It is not contrary to some in the contemporary church, a simple act of appointment or designation. Because it is a liturgical act, it is a celebration of the entire church, namely "the holy people united and arranged under their bishops" (SC, 26). Because it is a liturgical act, the full and active participation by all the people is the aim to be considered above all else (SC, 14). As is true of all liturgical acts, "each person, minister, or layman who has an office to perform, should carry out all and only those parts which pertain to his office by the nature of the rite and the norms of the liturgy"(SC, 28). By custom, tradition, and indeed law, the presiding celebrant of the liturgy of ordination is the bishop himself.

There is something privileged about liturgical acts presided over by the bishop. What this is, is named for the eucharist in the General Instruction to the Roman Missal (GI): "among the different ways of celebrating Mass in the local church, the most important, because the most meaningful, is that wherein the bishop presides over his priests and other ministers with the people taking their full and active part. This is the way in which the church is most clearly and visibly manifested" (GI, IV, 74). It is because this form of celebrating the eucharist most clearly presents the fullness of the church, and therefore the fullness of the mystery of Christ made present in the church (SC, 2), that it may be called the normative eucharist, against which all other celebrations of the eucharist should be measured and judged.

The liturgy of ordination properly takes place in the context of this normative eucharist. This observation provides a way out of a dilemma that has long afflicted the theology of orders, and that continues to surface in the contemporary church. It is phrased in either/or terms. Is the movement from Christ to the apostolic office and *then* to the church or from Christ to the church and *then* to the apostolic office? Clearly a different theology and praxis of orders will arise in each. The first will see orders as the passing on of powers received directly from Christ and handed on only by those who themselves possess the power. Under the principle that one cannot give what one has not received, only bishops could ordain bishops; bishops and in some circumstances presbyters could ordain presbyters; bishops, presbyters, and deacons could presumably ordain deacons. The Roman Catholic position is of course, that only bishops can ordain all three, born of the unity among the three orders and the fact that presbyter and deacon both assist and share in the episcopal ministry. The second theology would see apostolic office as arising from the church, even to the point of imagining that, in the absence of a bishop, presbyters could call a bishop forth from among themselves and in the absence of a priest, the laity could call a priest forth from among themselves.

The problem arises from a false premise: that church and Christ and apostolic office are three distinct entities, related only extrinsically. It is the same problem that was discussed above under the section on *essence,* the dilemma that results when essence is taken to be the same as entity. The problem is avoided when we remember that the church and the apostolic office are born together, in one and the same institutional act, each originating in the mystery of Christ who remains present at the depth of each.

In regard to the priesthood of the ordained and the priesthood of the baptized, it has been asserted that each brings forth the other, and this necessarily so as rooted in a deep truth of the mystery of Christ's own priesthood. It cannot activate itself from within itself. It must be drawn out by another. This is clear in the ministry of the ordained exercised toward the priesthood of the baptized. It is less clear how, and what it means that, the priesthood of the baptized brings forth the priesthood of the ordained. Until, that is, ordination as a liturgical act is properly located within the normative enactment of the eucharist.

Here is the perfect icon of mutual bringing-forth. At the

liturgy of ordination the bishop as presider calls forth the assembly of the church. The assembled church in turn calls forth the ministry of the bishop, asking him to ordain those of its members who are presented for ordination. Bishop calls forth the priesthood of the church; the church calls forth the priesthood of the bishop. Together, and in mutual interaction, they call forth the priesthood of Jesus Christ.

At this normative act of eucharist, presided over by the bishop and involving the full participation of all the faithful, the church at the fullest expression of its own deepest truth calls forth ordained bishops, presbyters and deacons. The bishop is essential, not because of the principle of *nemo dat quod non habet,* but because without him as presiding celebrant the fullest expression of the church is not made visible. It is a secondary question, though one not without its own importance, whether the bishop could delegate a presbyter or even a deacon to act in his stead. In principle it would seem possible, though it would not be liturgically ideal. Clear signification, or at least the fullest signification, of the unity of the whole church and its apostolic office in the one mystery of Jesus Christ would be lacking. However that question might be elsewhere pursued, what is most important here is to capture the unity of the two modes of Christ's priesthood in this one liturgical act where the fullness of the Church and fullness of the mystery of Christ, one and the same reality, is brought to visible and tangible expression.

The Ministry and Life of the Ordained

The liturgy of ordination for bishop, presbyter and deacon alike invokes the Holy Spirit upon those being ordained *for the sake of the ministry* they will perform. It would seem, at first glance at least, that it is only the ministries themselves that are affected by the consecration. It would seem, at first glance, that the persons themselves are touched by the prayer of consecration only when actually engaged in the ministries that are assigned. If indeed the ministries assigned were such as to require only skills (in preaching, in presiding, in governing and being pastor) that could be set in motion for the ministry and elsewhere set aside, this would indeed be true. The ministries are such, however, that more is required than skills.

One cannot preach unless one's whole life is conformed to the word one preaches. Conversely, one cannot preach without having one's whole life affected by the word one preaches. In a similar way, one cannot lead others into the prayer of Christ unless one's whole life is conformed to that prayer of Christ. Conversely, one cannot lead people in the prayer of Christ without having one's whole life affected by the prayer one prays. Finally, one cannot shepherd with the affection of Christ the Shepherd unless one's whole life is conformed to those affections. Conversely, one cannot shepherd with the affection of Christ the Shepherd without having one's whole life affected by the affections themselves. Ordained ministry incarnates the priesthood of Jesus Christ in the minister himself. The transformation through ordination cannot be restricted to the ministry alone, as if such were but occasional tasks to fulfill. The transformation through ordination involves the whole life of the minister because of the nature of the ministries themselves.

What remains to the task set at the beginning of these reflections is to draw out for the ministry and life of the ordained some descriptive notes of the way in which Christ's own priesthood manifests itself for the service of the church. In light of what has been developed thus far, three terms can serve this task: *embodiment, entrustment,* and *mutual iconography.*

(a) *Embodiment*

The truth of the church is that Christ continues to live and work within it. The truth of Christ himself is that he continues to be the Incarnate Christ, serving men and women through human, bodily interaction. The truth of Christ and the church is that the human church provides the bodily interaction while Christ himself effects through that bodily interaction his own saving work. The church is and remains *sacramentum Christi* in this sense.

For Christ to gather the church into his own prayer, sacrifice and saving mission, he requires that some provide him with a human body for the task. He requires that some be set in relation to the many and humanly enact his own relationship to them. He requires, in other words, *embodiment* in the church.

The human ministers who are asked by Christ-in-church to speak his word, call people into his prayer, and present his own pastoral care to his flock, are asked to give over their own human lives, indeed their own humanity, to the mission which Christ continues to fulfill. Through their humanity Christ will carry on his own triple task of announcing "good news," associating men and women to himself, and guiding men and women with the affections that are proper to a Good Shepherd.

For the ministers themselves, this can only be an act of love, and can only be born and nourished in a relationship with Christ that invites the surrender of one's own human life into the mission which he himself sets. Unless it is called forth by Christ in love, it will be a surrender into destruction. Only when it is called forth by Christ in love can it be a surrender into life.

Yet the Christ who calls forth this surrender of the few is not other than the Christ whose body is the church. A dangerous separation will result, and a dangerous form of Docetism, if Christ is imagined as other than embodied in the church. Inevitably, Christ will be set up over against the church as one who must be protected from the people of the church. It is with profound insight into the Incarnate Christ and the church as Christ's own body, that the bishop is advised at his ordination to "listen willingly" to the people of the church (Instruction). It is from there, embodied in his church, that Christ calls forth the priesthood of the ordained. It is to Christ in them that the ordained are asked to give their lives in love.

In the mutual interaction of ordained and baptized, there is no "third entity" to be negotiated. Two faces of the one priesthood of Christ, two *embodiments* of the one priesthood of Christ, call forth each other so that Christ himself may be unveiled in each. The people embody the Christ who calls forth the ordained. The ordained embody the Christ who calls the baptized to himself.

(b) *Entrustment*

This willingness of the ordained to see in the people the Christ who is calling their own priesthood forth, and conversely, of the people themselves to surrender to the ministry of the ordained, is a willingness that can only be rooted in both faith and hope. The humanity of the church can all too easily seem to be a threat to the truth of Christ, as the humanity of the ordained can all too often seem to be a hindrance to the presence of Christ. Human sinfulness does seem to mar this otherwise splendid picture of Christ in his church.

An old sacramental tradition addressed this when the issue was the sinfulness of the priest and its effect on sacramental effectiveness. Its bottom line, captured in the two noble phrases, *ex opere operato* and *ex opere operantis,* was this: do what the church, that is, Christ, intends and put no obstacle in the way. The point then was that the priest should do the former and the people the latter. It is a tradition that today could be called on as applying in its entirety both to the ordained and the baptized. Yet it is a tradition, whether old or new, that reaches beyond the evidence into the arena of trust.

The mystery of the one priesthood of Christ as it comes to expression in thee two different, yet mutually related and dependent modes, is that each must trust the Christ who is in the other. Without that trust the possibility of surrender and the possibility of being called foth will be damaged. Something must exist in the church to warrant that trust.

In the priesthood of Christ, as it was embodied first in the life of Jesus of Nazareth, surrender was made into the faithfulness of Abba, through the power of the Spirit which descended upon Jesus at his baptism. Here is the paradigm of both priesthood of ordained and priesthood of baptized. The firm covenant established by God in the life, death and resurrection of Jesus is the fidelity of God before whom and into whom persons are both baptized and ordained. The Spirit sent to consecrate and claim Jesus as "beloved Son," is the same Spirit invoked on baptized and ordained alike. The fidelity of God is that in which we hope; the Spirit of God is that which enables us to believe and trust.

The sacrament of orders is at its core an act of entrustment.

The Spirit is invoked upon those who are ordained. The people of the church entrust the ministries and ministers to that Spirit. The ministers themselves entrust themselves to that Spirit. It is a "holy conspiracy" enacted by the church, by which the ministers ordained will render human service, and the people of the church will receive human service, not as human service alone, but as bearers of the service, the presence and the power of Another, that is Christ. It is indeed far more than simple appointment or recognition of talents and gifts.

(c) *Mutual Iconography*

Sacramentality depends on visibility. I use the term *icon* here to name "that which is made visible." Throughout these reflections, we have referred to the priesthood of Christ made manifest, expressed, set forth in both the ordained and the baptized. Let me speak here of each being *icon* to the other.

If it were true that the ordained possessed power and possibility that the baptized could receive but not themselves possess, the ordained could serve as *icon* of Christ for the baptized, but the iconography would not be in any way mutual. The ordained would have to draw their own *icon* of Christ from another source. It is clear, however, in the vision of church set forth in Vatican II that this uni-directional view of priesthood is not in fact the case. Both the relationship that is essential between ordained and baptized, and their common rooting in the one priesthood of Christ, locate the power and possibility of Christ's own priesthood in each. Ordained serve as *icon* of Christ to the baptized, and baptized serve as *icon* of Christ for the ordained.

What does this mean in practice? A single example, from the ministry of forgiveness and reconciliation will serve to illustrate. In the former, the people are viewed as sinners in need of forgiveness and reconciliation. The priest is viewed as empowered and commissioned by Christ to forgive, with the Christ of the gospels serving as primary icon. The priest forgives, the people receive forgiveness, and the truth of Christ seems to be served. In the second, the "power of the keys" text from John (20:22-23) is joined to the witness of Paul: "All this is from God, who through Christ reconciled us to himself and gave us the ministry of reconciliation..." (II Cor 5:18). It is the need for forgiveness that summons the word of forgiveness from the ordained. Yet the very word of forgiveness spoken summons forth from the baptized that they too become for- givers and reconcilers to each other. The prayer of the Lord captures this mutuality well: "forgive us as we forgive...."

The point of the term *mutual iconography* is that, on the one hand, the power and possibility that lies hidden in the baptized, and yet which identifies their own true share in the priestly role and mission of Christ, is what the ordained must see, respond to and call forth in order to identify and properly carry out their own proper priesthood. On the other hand, the power and possibility that is set forth in the ministry and life of the ordained as they enact their own proper priesthood is what the baptized must call forth, see and respond to in order to identify and properly carry out their own proper priesthood. The priesthood of the ordained defines and makes manifest the priesthood of the baptized; the priesthood of the baptized defines and makes manifest the priesthood of the ordained.

Conclusion

A two-fold task was set at the beginning of these reflections: the theological task of *fides quaerens intellectum* and the pastoral task of deepening identity, purpose and mission in those already ordained or advancing toward ordination. The first has been accomplished. Whether successfully or not, adequately or not, is for the reader to judge. The second has likewise been accomplished, having developed along with the first. Again, to what success or adequacy, it is for the reader to judge.

One contemporary issue that was raised at the beginning concerned the loss in identity and purpose in regard to ordained priesthood that has resulted from the recovery of the priesthood of the baptized. The two are all too often taken to be in competition with each other. One conviction that has guided me in these reflections is that such competition is in the end detrimental to both. The two, as it were, "sink or swim" together. One cannot give importance to the priesthood of the baptized by diminishing priesthood of the ordained any more than one can give importance to the priesthood of the ordained by diminishing the priesthood of the baptized. Diminish one and you diminish both, and the priesthood of Christ itself is betrayed.

My aim here has been to advance the issue beyond competition into the mutuality and complementary of the two that the one priesthood of Christ requires. It has been, to be sure, to take the priesthood of the baptized as seriously as the documents of Vatican II mandate that we do. But it has been, as well, to take the priesthood of the ordained as seriously as the priesthood of Christ made manifest in both requires. Priesthood of the ordained requires not less attention than it received before the council; it requires perhaps even greater attention, and this not in spite of but precisely because of the priesthood of the baptized which has been given new emphasis in the church.

Is it worth giving a life to bring the priesthood of Christ alive in all the people of the church? Is it worth giving one's own humanity to be shaped by Christ's word, Christ's sacrifice, and Christ's own pastoral care of others? In the end the answer will only be given by those who "believe what they read, preach what they believe, and put into practice what they preach." By those who "know what they are doing, and imitate the mystery they celebrate." By those who shape their lives and their service according to the care and concern which the Good Shepherd has for all. In other words, the answer will only be given by those bishops, presbyters and deacons who say "yes."

Ordained Ministry:
Sign of Leadership and Unity
in the Great Sacrament of the Church

Robert Schwartz

Introduction

In the days after the Ascension the Christian community faced a very mysterious phenomenon: Jesus was no longer physically present in their midst, yet they experienced him in a new, pervasive and even more dynamic way than before. Having left them neither orphans to fend for themselves nor caretakers to tend the shop until he returned, Jesus continued to manifest himself within the Christian community. A fresh and exciting venture opened before their eyes as the Spirit led them to recognize the face of the risen Christ shining through the experience of the community of faith. A process of gestation had begun which would give birth, in time, to the sacramental spirituality of the Church.

Far from being absent, Jesus was now encountered continually in the concrete events of human life. The incarnation of Jesus and his passage through human life and death had sanctified the human realm, making it the place where God's face is revealed and men and women perfected. The risen body of the Lord was a guarantee that the human could indeed mediate the activity of God, and that what had begun in him was also happening to the brothers and sisters who made up his Body, the Church.

A theology of sacrament is not an abstraction, but an attempt to express the overwhelming experience of the Catholic tradition: Jesus manifests his presence and saving activity here and now through the community of faith. This conviction is expressed again in Vatican II's *Dogmatic Constitution on the Church*: "The Church, in Christ, is in the nature of a sacrament—a sign and instrument, that is, of communion with God and unity of the human race." (#1) Three dimensions of sacrament are highlighted: The Church is a sign or manifestation; it is an instrument; and it is both of these because it is "in Christ."

A number of theological concepts, usually not consciously related to one another in the tradition, speak about the sacramental self-understanding of the Christian community. Revelation, infallibility, transubstantiation and sacramental character all point to the same faith conviction—God has entered into a covenanted relationship with humanity, manifesting himself through human persons, endeavors and events, enabling them to be instruments of salvation.[1]

In order to further unwrap the point being made, let us briefly consider these three dimensions of a sacramental approach to the Church. Since the time of Abraham, and perhaps long before, God has used the human to reveal his presence. Abraham's journey of faith and the scriptural words which retell it are records of human experience, but they are also divine revelation. Tradition insists on the human character of the events and the text at the same time that it reverences the scriptures as the Word of God. The word "revelation" is an attempt to express a complex reality: human words manifest God; they are the instrument through which God saves. Finally, while the scriptures may remain unused or even be misused, they continue to be a promised place of encounter with the divine.

Tradition has understood other aspects of the Christian experience in a similar way. The doctrine of infallibility is an attempt to express the conviction of the faith community that it is more than a gathering of human beings, but in some mysterious way, it is also a manifestation and instrument of the divine, a recipient of God's enduring promise that "the gates of hell shall not prevail against it." Infallibility says more about God's faithfulness to the visible community he has called

[1] I am grateful to Fr. Peter Fink, S.J., of Weston School of Theology for his stimulating ideas in this area.

into existence than it does about the reliability of any office or institution.

Tradition believes that Christ is "substantially" present in the eucharist. What is being underlined again is the real and enduring relationship of God to a human reality. Manifestation, saving instrument and promise come together in the central act of fellowship and worship. The faithful believe that eucharistic eating and drinking is not only a human event or symbolic remembrance, but a real encounter with the Lord in his dying and rising. A word like "transubstantiation" testifies to the community's insight into the unique way in which the divine is covenanted to the human.

Sacramental character is an often maligned and misunderstood concept, facilely linked to human ontology and carelessly disassociated from the enduring faithfulness of God. Understood properly, it is another way of articulating the mysterious relationship of God to the human person. The baptized enter into a covenant with God, which on God's part is permanent and unbreakable. In this sense the baptized are marked by the divine in an indelible way, for God doesn't repent of promises. It is this relationship with the divine which empowers the baptized person to be both manifestation of God and instrument of salvation. The community believes that mission, too, arises from a covenant with God which adheres to the very being of the baptized through confirmation.

As a result, the mission of the laity does not come and go at the whim of the ordained, but is inherent in the initiated person. Sacramental character is an attempt to explain the way in which God has chosen to relate to the human person in a permanent way, enabling the person to be sign and minister of salvation.

The sacrament of orders stands in this same tradition. Ordained ministry is more than a set of functions; it is a unique manifestation and vehicle of the saving presence of God through the ministry of a covenanted person in a sacramental community.

This may seem like a long introduction to a discussion of ordained ministry; yet it is a very important one. The identity and mission of the ordained will be understood properly only when it is related to the sacramental insight which lies at the heart of the Catholic tradition. In other words, the best language for capturing the self-understanding of the Church is the language of sacrament. The distinctive character of ordained ministry must be sought within the self-understanding of the great sacrament of the Church.

Second Vatican Council

Vatican II very carefully places its treatment of ordained ministry within this self-understanding. Not until chapter 3 of the *Constitution on the Church* does it turn its attention to the hierarchy. In much the same way, the *Decree on the Ministry and Life of Priests* begins by stating that Christ "makes his whole Mystical Body sharer in the anointing of the Spirit wherewith he has been anointed ... therefore, there is no such thing as a member that has not a share in the mission of the whole Body."[2] The Council insists that the ordained be seen within the context of ecclesial life and as a distinctive expression of the nature of the Church.

In doing this, the phrase *in persona Christi*, in the person of Christ, or *in persona Christi, caput ecclesiae*, in the person of Christ the Head of the Church, is used in a technical sense. The Decree on Priests says: "The priesthood of priests, while presupposing the sacraments of initiation, is nevertheless conferred by its own particular sacrament. Through that sacrament, priests by the anointing of the Holy Spirit are signed with a special character and so are configured to Christ the priest in such a way that they are able to act in the person of Christ the head."[3]

The root of the tradition being invoked here goes back at least to Ignatius of Antioch:

---

[2] *Presbyterorum Ordinis* 2

[3] *Presbyterorum Ordinis* 2 This phrase or a near equivalent appears five times in the *Dogmatic Constitution on the Church*, three times in the *Decree on the Ministry and Life of Priests*, and once in the *Constitution on the Sacred Liturgy*. Vatican II uses this phrase only in conjunction with ordained ministry. Identification with Christ specifically as head of the Church is predicated only of the sacrament of orders.

> Wherever the bishop appears, the whole congregation is to be present, just as wherever Jesus Christ is, there is the whole Church. (Smyrn. 8; about A.D. 110)

Cyprian of Carthage wrote in a similar vein:

> Christ says to the apostles and thus to all of those placed in charge who now succeed to the apostles by delegated ordination: He who hears you, hears me: and he who hears me, hears him who sent me. (Ep 66,4; about A.D. 250)

> Certainly the priest who imitates that which Christ did and then offers the true and full Sacrifice ... according to what he sees Christ Himself offered, performs truly in the place of Christ. (Ep 63,14)

Cyprian is saying that Christ is present and active through the ordained, not that the ordained replace Christ. Another quotation makes that clear:

> You ought to know that the bishop is in the Church and the Church is in the bishop and, if there is anyone who is not with the bishop, he is not in the Church. . . . Look at length upon Christ, who by his will and Godhead and presence, governs both the leaders themselves and the Church *with* the leaders. (Ep 66,8-9)

The meaning of the phrase *in persona Christi* becomes clearer when viewed against the sacramental tradition of the Church. Like all sacraments, orders brings about a real presence of Christ. The *Constitution on the Sacred Liturgy* says that Christ is present in the Mass "in the person of his minister, 'the same now offering, through the ministry of priests, who formerly offered himself on the cross'."(#7) Thus the sacrament of orders manifests Christ, it extends his saving work, and it participates in his covenanted relationship with the Church.

The Good Shepherd

It must be remembered that the ordained do not exhaust the sacramental identity of the Church, but contribute to it by their own distinctive role. In explaining the sacramentality of ordained ministry, Vatican II points in two directions. Its first and primary emphasis is on the ordained as sign of Christ the servant head of the Church. As the sacrament of servant leadership, the role of pastor has pivotal significance—indeed, it is the overarching umbrella drawing together the various aspects of priestly ministry. The Council points to the eucharist as the source of pastoral charity and the summit and source of the community's life.

> By adopting the role of the good shepherd they (priests) will find in the practice of pastoral charity itself the bond of priestly perfection which will reduce to unity their life and activity. Now this pastoral charity flows especially from the eucharist.[4]

Although the leadership role of the pastor is wider than his liturgical functions, the eucharistic assembly reveals the various dimensions of presbyteral leadership at a high intensity moment in the life of the Church. In the hospitality of priests Christ the shepherd gathers his people. In their preaching the prophetic Christ speaks. Through their prayer of thanksgiving Christ involves all in his sacrifice to the Father and nourishes them at his table.

Each aspect of the saving work of Christ is important. Not to emphasize one at the expense of the others is a true discipline demanding balance, reflection, preparation and the development of skills. The Council focused priestly formation and spiritual development on pastoral leadership—described as shepherding, prophetic word and deed and leadership in prayer. The purpose of formation and spiritual growth is to

---

[4] *Presbyterorum Ordinis* 14.

provide a solid foundation capable of mediating the presence of Christ specifically as the servant leader of the People of God.

Priestly identity and spirituality do not stand apart from these pastoral functions, but in fact, are the implementation of a sacramental self-understanding. In other words, priests grow in holiness by becoming the leaders they were ordained to be. In the process of acting in the person of Christ, whether it be in the liturgy or in a wide range of pastoral activities, priests are offered the grace of conformity to the Christ they represent. Vatican II insists that priests grow in holiness, not in spite of ministry, but through the experience of it.

The realization that the ordained are sacramental persons in a very specific sense is the key to appropriate formation. The ability to lead is pivotal to an effective sacramental identity— yet not leadership in a worldly sense, but as Christ did it, through incarnation in the human dilemma and self-sacrificing service of those he came to save. Appropriate leadership skills must be tempered by human experience and transformed by self-transcendence.

The ordained are to take on the image of the Good Shepherd who was courageous leader, whole-hearted participant, mangled victim and risen victor. The blend of these testifies that Jesus is witness to God and not simply an example of good leadership skills. By growing in them the ordained become convincing signs of Christ. Activity changes people; the identity claimed in prayer becomes reality only when practiced in life. Prayer and ministry taken together change the self-understanding of priests.

In the same way, the preached word and preparation for the ministry of preaching has the power to shape the preacher, transforming him into the prophetic word he proclaims. Leadership in prayer immerses the presider in the liturgy, inviting conformity to the One he represents. In all of this, a sacramental identity is being honed. In acting in the person of Christ the head of the Church, the ordained are empowered to grow as sacraments through which Christ himself leads his people.

Although People of God is the image of the Church most

often associated with Vatican II, a vision of the Church as a communion of the faithful, united, enlivened and empowered by the common Spirit in baptism, is of greater theological significance and holds greater promise for revitalization of the Christian community.[5] Indeed, it is as sign and instrument of unity or communion that the Church is presented by the Council. In a community of equal persons exercising diverse ministries, the ordained perform a pivotal ministry as those who serve the unity of the members. In this context, a second way of looking at the sacramentality of ordained ministry is suggested, ever so slightly, in the Council documents.

In recognizing the dignity and responsibility of the laity, the bishops acknowledged an established fact. God has worked powerfully through the baptized in every age. The image of Christ the head, taken by itself, tends to concentrate attention on the clergy as source and mediators of grace. Concentration on concrete Christological images like head and body is typical of the Western Church. The Roman inclination toward structure and organization is easily expressed through the language of the body.

Eastern Tradition

The Eastern Church's love for Trinitarian spirituality offers liberating possibilities for a contemporary Church in which hierarchy and equality are often seen as incompatible. Viewed from a Trinitarian perspective, the work of salvation involves the collaboration of equal persons in diverse ways in a common saving mission. Collaboration does not prevent Jesus from submitting himself to the will of the Father, nor from claiming equality with him.

The Spirit unites the Father and the Son in the expression of their common mission. The Spirit is the primal gift which gives birth to the Church, producing there the image of the

---

[5]For an excellent study on the significance of *communio* in contemporary ecclesiology see Gene S. Scapanski, *The Role of the Laity in the Context of Communio and Mission*, doctoral dissertation: Pontifical University of St. Thomas Aquinas (Angelicum), 1988.

Trinity: equality of persons, unity in mission and diversity of roles. In short, grace produces a collaborative community which mirrors its divine source.

In this scheme of things the ordained are sacraments of the Spirit binding the diverse ministries of the Church into one community with a common mission. Thus, they have an essential role to play in the ordering of the Church. It is to this that the Council points:

> While trying the spirits if they be of God, they (priests) must discover with faith, recognize with joy, and foster with diligence the many and varied charismatic gifts of the laity, whether these be of a humble or more exalted kind....
> Priests have been placed in the midst of the laity so that they may lead them all to the unity of charity.... Theirs is the task, then, of bringing about agreement among divergent outlooks in such a way that nobody may feel a stranger in the Christian community. They are to be defenders of the common good.... (Ministry and Life of Priests #9)

Finding themselves in a Church of many ministries, the ordained are called to collaboration with others and to the exercise of the ministry which is distinctively their own—care for the unity of the Church. This means binding the community to its apostolic origins, securing its relationship to the universal Church and safeguarding harmony among its ministries.

Sacrament of Unity

The Eucharistic Preface for Christian Unity points to the Spirit's role in both the diversity and unity of the Church:

> How wonderful are the works of the Spirit, revealed in so many gifts! Yet how marvelous is the unity the Spirit creates from their diversity, as he dwells in the hearts of your children, filling the whole Church with his presence and guiding it with his wisdom!

The ordained are to exercise a ministry of unity as sacramental manifestations of the Spirit's presence.

While our consciousness of the diversity of gifts and ministries within the community has grown in the wake of the Council, the unifying ministry of the bishop is an ancient one, as Ignatius of Antioch testifies:

> Therefore it is fitting that you should live in harmony with the will of the bishop, as indeed you do. For your justly famous presbytery, worthy of God, is attuned to the bishop as the strings to a harp.... Now do each of you join in this choir, that being harmoniously in concord you may receive the key of God in unison, and sing with one voice through Jesus Christ to the Father.... (Ign. Eph. 4,1-2)

The exhortation of Vatican II is nuanced a bit differently; there the emphasis is on the ordained actively seeking harmony in the community and not only on the community finding unity in agreement with the will of the bishop.

If the ordained are a sacrament of unity and harmony in a collaborative mission, then becoming who they were ordained to be, demands relational skills, courage, patience and trust in a multiplicity of gifts beyond their own. A vision of themselves as unifiers which is born in prayer must be tested in the give-and-take of community life, especially in moments of tension and division. The ordained minister must stand in the midst of the typical liberal-conservative or social action-prayer divisions in today's Church, not to take sides, but to serve the greater truth which unites people across their differences. By definition, the ordained person is not partisan to a particular ideology, but a servant of the common good.

These two images of the ordained are not presented as options in Vatican II, but as complementary aspects of a unified presbyteral mission. In fact, the combination of the two offers a rich picture of the role of the priest in the Church today. While too constricted an interpretation of headship could lead to clerical dominance, too much emphasis on a

unifying role could lead to a presbyterate of congenial person-
alities who add little of substance to people's lives.

In fact, priests are not only to bring about unity, but they
are also to empower, to nurture and to enable the ministry of
others. Seen in this light, the role of the head is not to control,
but to evoke the body's full potential by mediating the Spirit
who enlightens, inspires, challenges, supports and brings gifts
to birth in the members. This is an active role which moves far
beyond co-ordination. Because the Spirit acts in relationship
to Christ, the head truly has a relationship to gifts in the
members. So, too, the ordained not only lead and unify, but
they also mediate the Spirit who empowers the community.

The Council's admonition that the ordained are to discern
and recognize the gifts of the Spirit in the laity, and its
suggestion that they may even be joyfully surprised by what
they see, doesn't suggest that these gifts happen apart from
their ministry. In fact, it is through preaching, baptism and the
eucharist that the ordained mediate an experience of the Spirit—
yet, this does not imply that they control the results or that
they are not amazed by the outcome. As sacrament of Christ
and his Spirit, the ordained person exercises the complex
ministry of bringing the body to full maturity. This involves
birthing, nurturing, uniting, leading and liberating the people
of God. Through ordained ministry exercised by frail human
beings, Christ continues to build up the great sacrament of the
Church; by his Spirit, shared in complementary ways by laity
and clergy, he leads it in its mission to the world.

Conclusion

In summary, a contemporary theology of ordained ministry
must build on the following insights:

1) Ordained ministry embodies an essential and unique
aspect of the self-understanding of the Church. Language
which describes the Church as communion, mission and sacrament must also be applied to ordained ministry if it is to be
understood and lived in a way which corresponds with the
theology flowing from Vatican II.

2) The Christian community's insight into the on-going

presence and activity of Christ in the world through the mediation of human persons, gatherings and events is the key to understanding the sacramentality of the total Church, and of ordained ministry within it. Language of stewardship, or ministry through stand-ins or vicars in the Lord's absence, is inadequate to explain the reality. The faith community believes that Christ himself acts through the Church as a whole and through a myriad of ministries and charisms within it. An accurate theology of ordained ministry must flow from an understanding of the Church as sacrament and the ordained as sacramental persons within it.

3) The Council's use of the phrase *in persona Christi* is sacramental in purpose. The primary interpretation of this phrase in the documents of Vatican II is that of sacrament of Christ, the head of the Church. To be faithful to the intent of the Council, headship must be understood as it exists in Christ, that is, as ongoing incarnation in the human venture and self-sacrificing service to human need.

4) A contemporary theology of ordained ministry must be significantly influenced by the Council's endorsement of an ecclesiology of communion based on the common mission bestowed in baptism. The recognition of gifts, dispersed among the faithful and of the ordained as servants of the common good offers the bare bones of a more collaborative approach to ministry and renewed insight into the unifying role of the ordained. Full recovery of an understanding of ordained ministry as sacrament of the unifying Spirit rests on both the unfolding of a Trinitarian spirituality and the interaction of established and emerging ministries. An appreciation of the Church as the embodiment of Trinitarian relationships—as the living out of grace—is crucial to the healthy development of the Catholic tradition.

5) It is essential that the two ways of looking at the sacramentality of ordained ministry be seen as complementary and necessarily related to one another. If this is not done, ordained ministry will take on a too dominant role, on one hand, or a merely auxiliary role on the other. A balanced approach to the presbyteral mission, which sees priests both as mediators of the Spirit's presence and as unifiers of the work of the Spirit in others, is indispensable.

The Mystery of the Priestly Vocation

J. Francis Stafford, D.D.
Archbishop of Denver

I. The Mystery of the Church

The years since the Second Vatican Council have been a time of excitement and turbulence in the Roman Catholic Church. An extraordinary pastoral renewal has taken place in our midst: The liturgy has been reformed, the Scriptures have assumed a greater prominence in our lives, the people of God have dedicated themselves anew to the life of holiness to which we are all called, religious are seeking to resummon the charism of their respective founders and foundresses, the hierarchical ministry has recalled its evangelical and collegial foundations, and everywhere the church has sought to realize a dialogue within the human community—the vision of Pope John XXIII and Pope Paul VI, which the council made its own. It has been a time of inspiration and hard work filled with the signs of the Spirit, who protects us and leads us forward. Seldom has history seen a community as vast or as ancient as the Roman Catholic Church change as dramatically or as fast.

Yet the very sources of that excitement have also at times given rise to a certain anxiety among us, since change is never easy for human beings. Honesty compels us to admit that renewal has had its price: disillusionment and discouragement for some, contention and divisiveness for many, and for most of us, at one time or another, a disorientation and bewilderment concerning an outcome we simply cannot yet see.

In few areas of the church's life is this ambiguity as deep as in the ministry. Bishops and priests have discovered a new meaning in their call as a reinvigorated people of God take up the council's challenge to evangelize. The permanent diaconate has been restored and with it the ministerial symbolism of a sacramental ministry by married men. Parochial ministry has been diversified, and many well-trained associates, men and women, religious and lay, have stepped forward to serve the church in cooperation with pastors and bishops. But exciting as these developments have been, they have also seen their trying moments. In some places there is confusion about roles and accountability. Almost everywhere the dwindling number of priests is becoming a serious concern, and the most troubling report about the ministry is that priests themselves are no longer asking suitable candidates to consider a priestly vocation—in effect, no longer recruiting their own replacements.

This pastoral letter is one of several which I intend to offer in the hope of affording some clarity and direction in the present ecclesial context of excitement, ambiguity and turmoil. I anticipate offering on later occasions some thoughts on the recruitment of vocations to the priesthood and on the growing phenomenon of lay ministry. In this letter, just the same, I will reflect on the mystery itself of the ordained priesthood. In the considerations that follow, I will proffer more a review of doctrine than a speculative treatise. I will recall the connection of priesthood and sacrifice, especially as it is signified in the new covenant, and I will recall the central role played in that new covenant by the priestly mediation of Christ. Then I will develop the distinction and relation of the two orders of sacramental symbolism by which the priesthood of Christ continues in the church: the universal priesthood of the baptized and the ordained priesthood of the presbyter. Finally, in developing the latter idea, I will emphasize the essential note of the ordained ministry, the capacity to act *in persona Christi*, in the person of Christ, the head of the body. The priest is set apart within the church by his priestly consecration, and this to render service to others; yet he is first called for this consecration from among the members of the church, the body of Christ, and he ever afterward remains a part of their life.

These reflections must necessarily be limited in scope. While I intend to review some of the elements that are essential to understanding and living the priestly ministry, I cannot review all of them. Moreover, the priesthood itself is understood and lived in a variety of ways, which I cannot do justice here by describing them. Let me at least, nonetheless, affirm the manifold embodiments of the priestly mystery which we find in the secular and religious priests of the archdiocese. I know well that a fundamental unity links these embodiments to the unique priesthood of Christ, thus to one another and to the church. I know too that precisely through this variety the presbyterate as a whole realizes the pastoral strategy of St. Paul: to be "all things to all men" (1 Cor. 9:22), to continue the saving work of the Redeemer, I am continually edified in my work as archbishop with these priests, and I daily ask the Lord to bless them and their priestly ministry.

My prayer in offering these reflections to the archdiocese is that the Lord grant to us all, especially to us priests, a "wisdom of heart" (see Ps. 90) concerning the priestly consecration, a wisdom not unlike that which Solomon sought for his own royal office (1 Kgs. 3:9; Wis. 9:1-18). I pray that the Lord grant us a wisdom of the priesthood as practical, farseeing and keenly discerning as the wisdom of Solomon, and as loving, generous and humbly service oriented as the mind of Christ Jesus. And I pray that the Lord grant to priests themselves a renewal of the Spirit of holiness whom the bishop invoked at their ordination: a true molding into the likeness of Christ, the supreme and eternal priest.

The church is a mystery whose life derives from the supreme mystery that is the triune God. As Pope Paul VI said in his opening allocution at the second session of the Second Vatican Council:

> The church is a mystery. It is a reality imbued with the hidden presence of God. It lies, therefore, within the very nature of the church to be always open to new and greater exploration.

This God has graciously willed to share his very life with us in a dialogue by which he has gradually made himself known to us and invited us to accept his friendship. When, through his grace, we accept that friendship, our sins are healed and we are elevated to a new life. In fact we are elevated to the level of the divine, to take part in that ineffable mystery of intimacy and love which constitutes the inner life of the Trinity.

As St. John the Evangelist teaches us, "No one has ever seen God" (1:18); but the Son has made God known to those whom the Father has given him (17:6). John also teaches us that no one can come to the Father except through the Son, who is the way (14:6). The Son is, as the Letter to the Hebrews says, the great high priest who entered once for all into the heavenly sanctuary that he might appear before God on our behalf (9:11, 24). He is the high priest who lives forever to make intercession for those who approach God through him (7:23)—the high priest who assures our entrance into that heavenly sanctuary by the new and living path which he has opened for us (10:19).

Through Christ we have access in one spirit to the Father (Eph. 2:18); for it is through this Spirit that we belong to Christ and have the adoption that makes us children of God and heirs with Christ (see Rom. 8:9, 14-17). So closely are we joined to Christ, that we are said to be one spirit with him (1 Cor. 6:17), living now not our own lives, but Christ's (see Gal. 4:20). As the church celebrates in its eucharistic liturgy, we live this new life in Christ in such a way that we share his divinity as he shared our humanity (second prayer at the preparation of gifts)—indeed, in such a way that the Father sees and loves in us what he sees and loves in Christ (Preface VII, Sundays in ordinary time). More important, through the Spirit the Father draws all things to Christ (Jn. 6:44) until that sublime moment when Christ, having received the subjection of all things, will in turn subject himself to the Father so that God may be all in all (1 Cor. 15:28).

Lumen Gentium, the Dogmatic Constitution on the Church of the Second Vatican Council, compares the church to the mystery of the Incarnate Word. "As the assumed nature, inseparably united to him, serves the divine Word as a living organ of salvation, so in a somewhat similar way does the social structure of the church serve the Spirit of Christ who vivifies it, in the building up of the body" (No. 8, referring to Eph. 4:15).

The church is a complex reality comprised of the human and the divine: a visible, structured community and yet an invisible participation in the life of Trinity; a concrete, even weakness-filled group of human beings in time and history, and a mystical communion transcending time through the mediatorship of its Redeemer. The church may seem ordinary, everyday and routine, yet its life is the mystery of communion with Christ just described. This mysterious communion is such that through Christ we go to the Father and through us Christ is heard (Lk. 10:15), Christ is accepted (Jn. 13:20) and Christ is welcomed (Mt. 10:40) by the world he came to save. For Christ specifically commissioned his church to go forth and bear fruit that will endure (Jn. 15:16), sending it as he himself was sent (Jn. 20:21) to make disciples of all the nations (Mt. 28:19).

A. Mystery as such

It is the character of mystery to elude full grasp by our mastery or intelligence—and this more for the richness which it encompasses than for the poverty of our abilities. This elusive character belongs to mysteries which we do not ordinarily even consider supernatural. Existence itself is a mystery and is not simply another problem to be solved as science and technology might lead us unsuspectingly to assume.

There is no question that scientific research has yielded the possibility for a safer, healthier, more productive, more comfortable human environment. But scientific research is often detached, impersonal and abstract in character. Furthermore, there are some aspects of reality which scientific reflection cannot even hope to touch: love, fidelity, hope, compassion, honor, endurance, integrity, courage, sacrifice—in short, the very qualities that give our humanity its greatest dignity. For these, a different type of reflection is required, for they cannot be approached in a detached manner. We must first know them by our experience of them, by our participating in them for ourselves. Another person may testify to us concerning them, but it remains for each of us to discover them on our own. Thus, prior to scientific thought, one must engage in another type of reflection in which what is known is inseparable from the way in which we have come to know it: a type of reflection in which the truth discovered is also a truth of which we are part. As in music or drama or art, the meaning which is discovered upon this type of reflection cannot be simply restated apart from the medium in which it is embodied. Indeed, this reflection would compel us to treat our very life and its mysteries with a greater reverence than that shown to a priceless work of art.

Often our attitude toward the mystery of faith has defined it merely as a revealed truth which we cannot fully understand in this life, but can expect to understand in the next. But this approach defines mystery too narrowly in terms of our reason, too broadly in comparison with science, with its emphasis on one's ability to attain mastery. Divine mystery should be described instead in relation to a different type of human capacity or faculty altogether. It should be described in a way more primordial than the distinction between knowledge and love, because it contains them both. Thus what is essential in our relation to mystery is not that we can or cannot fully know it, but that we can lovingly live in its presence—now in its shadow, then in its light, never fully comprehending its overflowing love.

Ultimately there is only one mystery: God. The Trinity that is God's life is the central mystery that unifies the whole of divine revelation and orders our response to him. God is a community of persons in one nature, and we are created in his image. More wonderfully, God has called us to share by means of grace, and eventually by vision, in his Trinitarian community, to share in the divine inner life of love. Through salvation history God has revealed this destiny to us in a series of interventions that constitute the economy of salvation. Thus God "has given us the wisdom to understand fully the mystery, the plan he was pleased to decree in Christ" (Eph. 1:9).

In the New Testament, especially in the writings of St. Paul, mystery is overwhelmingly a matter of God's historical plan to reveal himself in Christ Jesus and so to reconcile all things to himself. This mystery, God's hidden wisdom, distinct from the wisdom of any given age, is revealed to the church through the Spirit, who searches the depths of God, and it can be known only by the spiritually mature (1 Cor. 2:6-16). As that wisdom is expressed in Christ and the cross, it is absurdity to the worldly, but in fact it overturns their version of wisdom, "for the foolishness of God is wiser than human wisdom, and the weakness of God is stronger than human strength" (1 Cor. 1:25).

B. Mystery and Apostolic Office

For St. Paul too an intrinsic part of the mystery is the manner in which God has chosen for it to be manifest. The mystery is not revealed all at once and for everyone, but it must be communicated from its recipients to others by word of mouth and by the power of the Spirit; this is the process of evangelization, or preaching the Gospel. It is clear too that St. Paul understood that the apostles were commissioned to a particular position and authority in this process. As he reminded the Ephesians: "When you read what I have said, you will realize that I know what I am talking about in speaking of the mystery of Christ, unknown to men in former ages but now revealed by the Spirit to the holy apostles and prophets" (Eph. 3:4-5).

Indeed the whole of St. Paul's writing shows his self-awareness of possessing a special function (*munus*) in the church, as he enlightened, exhorted, encouraged, admonished, sanctified and interceded for the churches which he had visited or, for the greater part, had founded.

Lumen Gentium notably adopts as its own the general New Testament notion of mystery, declaring that in the life of the church the persons of the Trinity extend salvation history even to our day. The constitution describes the mystery of the church using the biblical images of sheepfold, cultivated field, vineyard, house, temple, city, mystical body—all in a type of poetic reflection. But even when considering the church in the most generic terms, as simply "mystery," the constitution insists on the uniqueness of the apostolic office as part of that mystery:

> There is only one Spirit who, according to his own richness and the needs of the ministries, gives his different gifts for the welfare of the church (cf. 1 Cor. 12:1-11). Among these gifts, the primacy belongs to the grace of the apostles to whose authority the Spirit himself subjects even those who are endowed with charisms (cf. 1 Cor. 14) (No. 7).

Thus the apostolic office, and its continuation through the centuries in the episcopacy, in the priesthood and in their interrelationship, is intrinsic to the mystery of the church and shares in the church's nature of mystery. Like the church, the structure of the apostolic office cannot be fully and finally subject to scientific or technocratic questioning and problem solving even though the effort to understand the office better and to implement it more effectively can never cease. Since the apostolic office itself is a mystery, it must primarily be approached with that other type of reflection to which I adverted earlier.

Such an approach, for instance, can be found in the church's liturgy, where the apostolic office celebrated with holy reverence and gratitude as a gift of Christ to his church. The liturgical calendar contains feasts in honor of the apostles, celebrating them as the inspired first preachers and guardians of the Gospel who ultimately testified to their conviction of its truth by giving their lives. Above all, in these liturgical occasions, the church remembers and celebrates "the Eternal Shepherd, who never leaves his flock untended" (Preface of the Apostles, I) as well as the incarnational nature of Christ's pastoral care for his flock—a care continuously embodied in the successors of the apostles, the bishops, along with the co-workers of the latter, the priests.

A similar approach to the apostolic office is contained in the very structure of liturgical ceremonies themselves: in the appointed liturgical roles of bishops and priests; in their vesture, placement and gesture; in their being reverenced with bows or with incense. Perhaps the most moving celebration of the apostolic office occurs in the ceremonies of ordination, in which a variety of ancient rites of taking office are applied to those being ordained in order to symbolize their being assimilated to a new role before God and in the church.

II. The Mystery of the Priesthood

To bring this whole discussion of mystery to focus on the priest, the simplest thing to say is that he is a man of mystery. While he is called forth from among the members of the church and ever remains human and a sinner, he is nonetheless set apart for sacred duty and thus is permanently marked with a special character. He becomes by that which he has been marked a special participant in the continuing drama of salvation (1 Cor. 15:9-10). When the priest is serious about the holiness and pastoral charity which this character requires, a spontaneous respect and even reverence of him is present in the church. His priestly character has become more intensely visible. He himself is a symbol.

Christians bear the name of Christ and must manifest him to the world. Yet who is to manifest Christ to the Christian? The Roman Catholic Church is not a leaderless assembly which waits until a spontaneous inspiration is given to one among them. Since the need for such inspiration and leadership is an abiding one, "Christ the Lord instituted in his church a variety of ministries which work for the good of the whole body," including "those ministers who are endowed with sacred power" (*Lumen Gentium*, 18).

So in a special way the priest is a reflection of Christ within the church. Like Jesus himself, who was "a man like us in all things but sin" (Eucharistic Prayer IV), the priest will reflect solidarity with his people, express compassion for them and be empathetic with them. Throughout the years the pastoral practice of Catholic priests in the United States has reflected well this solidarity. Perhaps as a consequence of generations of work—religious, social and political—within the various Catholic immigrant communities priests have enjoyed a degree of closeness to their people not often found elsewhere.

But again, like Jesus himself, who was the Christ, the Son of God, a priest will also somehow reflect the otherness of the holy. He is not just "one of the guys." Although he is always a brother, he is also set apart for others, and he is called in some way, however seemingly impossible, to embody the transcendence of God as well as his immanence, his awesomeness and his closeness. If the Catholic priest is at once the Christ of the banquet table—familiar, convivial, feasting with outcasts and sinners, he is also, by the grace of God, the Christ of Mount Tabor, transfigured, glorious, translucent of the divine—however obscure that embodiment may be.

Recent pastoral practice of Catholic priests in the United States seems to reflect a difficulty with this second aspect of the priestly mission. Perhaps the egalitarianism and populism of American society and politics excessively reinforce a natural human reluctance before the enormity and challenge of this God-given role. But must not someone reflect to us that God's ways are not ours, that the All Holy deserves our reverence and awe as well as our love? In an incarnate church must we not have—as well as ministerial encounters that console and encourage us—encounters that leave us to ask, "Were not our hearts burning within us?" (Lk. 24:32).

A. *Priesthood and Sacrifice*

The apostolic letter of Pope John Paul II, *Dominicae Cenae*, of Feb. 24, 1980, reaffirmed the traditional link of the priesthood to the eucharist and of the eucharist to the notion of sacrifice:

> The eucharist is the principal and central *raison d'etre* of the sacrament of the priesthood, which effectively came into being at the moment of the institution of the eucharist, and together with it.

> The priest fulfills his principal mission and is manifested in all his fullness when he celebrates the eucharist and this manifestation is more complete when he himself allows the depth of that mystery to become visible, so that it alone shines forth in people's hearts and minds through his ministry (No. 2).

The priest is united in a particular way to the eucharist: In the pope's expression, he derives his existence from it and exists for it. The eucharist, in turn, bears a sacrificial character, to which the priest is therefore related:

> The eucharist is above all else a sacrifice. It is the sacrifice of the redemption and also the sacrifice of the new covenant.
>
> Consequently, the celebrant, as minister of this sacrifice, is the authentic priest, performing—in virtue of the specific power of sacred ordination—a true sacrificial act that brings creation back to God (No. 9).

In virtue of the specific power of sacred ordination, the priest in the eucharist renews the redemptive sacrifice of Christ and unites to it the offerings of the participants. But there is more to be said. In the humanity of those who offer the sacrifice—the participants, the priest, the Redeemer himself—the whole order of creation is summed up and symbolized: mineral, biological, psychological and spiritual. Therefore, in the eucharist, creation itself returns to the God from whom it has come.

In the popular religious imagination, the image of an Old Testament or pagan priest usually involves the activity of sacrifice. Whether Aaron, Zadok or the high priest of Thebes, he is almost always pictured with arms uplifted as smoke curls from the holocaust. In the new dispensation, the smoke has disappeared, and the priest and holocaust are the same: Jesus of Nazareth, the risen Lord and Christ, who bears in his glorified body the marks of his awesome passion, a sign that priest, victim and sacrifice live forever to save. In the Book of Revelation, we meet him: the Lamb, standing "as though slain" (5:6), who makes of us a "a kingdom and priests to serve our God" (5:10). He has offered a perfect sacrifice once for all; it will never be repeated. But he reaches across time into every succeeding age to draw us into that one perfect act, to make that act here and now present through the sacramental ministry of the priest. The church firmly believes that her Lord has willed his sacrifice to continue in her midst and that this same

Lord, in drawing her to himself, draws her into his "holy and living sacrifice" (Eucharistic Prayer III).

Because there is only one sacrifice in the new covenant, Christ is the one priest of the new covenant community. This is why Roman Catholic priests are said to possess the priesthood of Jesus Christ. It is not strictly speaking their priesthood, but his. It is not something which they do on their own, but something which he himself does through them.

B. The Universal Priesthood of the Baptized

Even before we speak of priests as such, however, there is a more encompassing sense in which Christ has willed his priesthood and sacrifice to continue in the church: in the universal or common priesthood of the baptized. It is sometimes referred to as the priesthood of the laity, but does not belong to the laity alone; it belongs to all the baptized, ordained priests and religious men and women included. It is the priesthood invoked by Preface 1 for Sundays of ordinary time, when the church celebrates its calling as "a chosen race, a royal priesthood, a holy nation, a people set apart." In this, the church simply repeats the words of the First Letter of St. Peter (2:9), who himself recalled the even more ancient prerogatives of Israel recited in the Book of Exodus, "You shall be to me a kingdom of priests, a holy nation" (19:6).

What is this universal priesthood of the baptized and how is the ordained priesthood related to it? *Lumen Gentium* answers the first part of this question as follows:

> The baptized, by regeneration and the anointing of the Holy Spirit, are consecrated to be a spiritual house and a holy priesthood, that through all the works of Christian men they may offer spiritual sacrifices and proclaim the perfection of him who has called them out of darkness into his marvelous light (cf. 1 Pt. 2:4-10). Therefore all the disciples of Christ, persevering in prayer and praising God (cf. Acts 2:42-47), should present themselves as a sacrifice, living, holy and pleasing to God (cf. Rom. 12:1) (No. 10).

Later, speaking of the universal priesthood as it is exercised specifically by the laity, the constitution adds:

> To those whom he intimately joins to his life and mission (Christ) also gives a share in his priestly office, to offer spiritual worship for the glory of the Father and the salvation of man. Hence the laity, dedicated as they are to Christ and anointed by the Holy Spirit, are marvelously called and prepared so that even richer fruits of the Spirit may be produced in them. For all their works, prayers and apostolic undertakings, family and married life, daily work, relaxation of mind and body, if they are accomplished in the Spirit—indeed even the hardships of life if patiently borne—all these become spiritual sacrifices acceptable to God through Jesus Christ (cf. 1 Pt. 2:5). In the celebration of the eucharist these may be most fittingly offered to the Father along with the body of the Lord. And so, worshipping everywhere by their holy actions, the laity consecrate the world itself to God (No. 34).

The concept that is found in both of these passages and that holds the key to understanding the universal priesthood is the notion of the spiritual sacrifice, a notion with roots in the Old Testament.

When the great prophetic movement began in Israel in the ninth century B.C., it appeared that traditional religion in the kingdoms of Israel and Judah had fallen on hard times. Kings, their courts and higher officialdom had gradually lost sight of the demands of the covenant, with the result that a situation of idolatry, injustice and ritualism ensued. The royal courts worshiped the gods of foreign-born nobility. The powerful became oppressors, with little care for the poor, neglected and needy. The religious rites of the temple as well as religious pratices such as fasting, while scrupulously observed in externals, came to have little internal meaning.

Into this situation the prophets were sent by God. Like a whirlwind they came, first demanding worship of the one God of Israel and second demanding a worship from the heart, an interiorized worship that would issue in works of justice and mercy. The eighth-century prophet Hosea simply expresses the idea in an oracle: "For it is love that I desire, not sacrifice, and knowledge of God rather than holocausts" (6:6). Psalm 50 expresses the same idea in a passage clearly influenced by the prophets:

> Not for your sacrifices do I rebuke you, for your holocausts are before me always. I take from your house no bullock, no goats out of your fold. If I were hungry, I would not tell you, for mine are the world and its fullness. Do I eat the flesh of strong bulls, or is the blood of goats my drink? Offer to God praise as your sacrifice and fulfill your vows to the Most High. He that offers praise as a sacrifice glorifies me; and to him that goes the right way, I will show the salvation of God   (8-9, 12-14, 23).

In other words, the prophets did not rebuke the rituals of sacrifice, but only the attitude by which participants in the ritual failed to realize internally the meaning of what they were doing.

The language of the internalization of worship in the sacrifice of praise has survived to our own day in the liturgy of the eucharist. Originally, this "sacrifice" may have been a simple psalm of praise offered by participants while their sacrificial gift was offered by the priest. It was their way of internalizing the external gesture of the ritual. But the prophets demanded more than the internalization of liturgical ritual; they demanded an internalization that expressed itself in the rest of one's life: by the observance of the commandments and by a generosity that reached out to the helpless. This broadened sense of sacrifice is the spiritual sacrifice of which St. Peter speaks in his first letter (2:5), of which the documents of the Second Vatican Council still speak, and which is still offered in the Roman liturgy of the eucharist, most expressly in Eucharistic Prayer 1.

Thus the universal priesthood is exercised in the day-to-day activity of the Christian life. In the case of the laity, *Lumen Gentium* makes this point even more strongly:

Their secular character is proper and peculiar to the laity.... By reason of their special vocation it belongs to the laity to seek the kingdom of God by engaging in temporal affairs and directing them according to God's will. They live in the world, that is, they are engaged in each and every work and business of the earth and in the ordinary circumstances of social and family life which, as it were, constitute their very existence. There they are called by God that, being led by the spirit of the Gospel, they may contribute to the sanctification of the world, as from within, like leaven, by fulfilling their own particular duties. Thus, especially by the witness of their life, resplendent in faith, hope and charity, they must manifest Christ to others. It pertains to them in a special way so to illuminate and order all temporal things with which they are so closely associated that these may be effected and grow according to Christ and may be to the glory of the Creator and Redeemer (No. 31).

It is perhaps because of this secular character that the universal priesthood is also referred to by the title of royal priesthood. The king after all was an anointed figure, but a layman, deeply involved in temporal affairs. In a similar way the royal priesthood of the baptized concerns the daily living out of an incarnate Christian life within time.

True, the royal priesthood is a sharing in the priestly kingship of Christ. However, we must also bear in mind the care and insistence with which Christ himself in the Gospels corrected his disciples' mistaken notions of kingship. This messiah, he challenged them, came to suffer and only in that way to enter his glory. He was to be rejected, not acclaimed. He came to serve, not to lord his authority over others. He insisted on making his way to victory by the power and authority of his own weapons: humility, obedience and poverty, not by the sword. Moreover, he made it clear to his disciples—and he makes it clear to us—that if rejection and misunderstanding were the treatment afforded him, we the disciples could expect the same. The universal priesthood of the baptized will be royal only in the manner of Christ, the shepherd king who laid down his life for the sheep. As St. Paul told the Philippians:

> Your attitude must be that of Christ: Though he was in the form of God, he did not deem equality with God something to be grasped at. Rather he emptied himself and took the form of a slave, being born in the likeness of men.
>
> He was known to be of human estate, and it was thus that he humbled himself, obediently accepting even death, death on a cross!
>
> Because of this, God highly exalted him and bestowed on him the name above every other name.
> So that at Jesus' name every knee must bend in the heavens, on the earth and under the earth, and every tongue proclaim to the glory of God the Father: Jesus Christ is Lord! (2:5-11).

III. The Distinctness of the Ordained Priesthood

Then how is the ordained priesthood distinct from the universal? In the formula of *Lumen Gentium*, it is distinct "in essence and not only by degree" (No. 10). The ordained priesthood is not simply a concentration of the universal priesthood nor is the ordained priest himself any sort of super-Christian. Rather, the ordained priesthood is an essential distinction in the life of the church by which the ordained priest himself bears a special mark of service within the church, becoming a Christian "set apart for the Gospel of God" (Rom. 1:1). Ordination does not separate the priest from the rest of the church, but indeed designates him in the midst of the church for a unique service to his brothers and sisters. The preface of the Chrism Mass, which is also used at the ordination of priests, celebrates this reality. In words of gratitude and praise addressed to the heavenly Father, the bishop prays:

> Christ gives the dignity of a royal priesthood to the people he has made his own. From these, with a brother's love, he

chooses men to share his sacred ministry by the laying on of hands. He appoints them to renew in his name the sacrifice of our redemption as they set before your family his paschal meal.

Through the ministry of the ordaining bishop, Christ shares his own priestly ministry with the ordinand, who is thus "taken from among men and appointed for men in the things which pertain to God, in order to offer gifts and sacrifices for sins."[1] Consequently, when the priest celebrates among God's family the redemptive sacrifice of the eucharist, he experiences and embodies what Pope John Paul II has called, in the document cited earlier, the *raison d'etre* of the priesthood. This is precisely the element that constitutes the distinctness of the ordained ministry.

The words of *Lumen Gentium* are forceful:

> The ministerial priest, by the sacred power which he possesses, forms and rules the priestly people; in the person of Christ he effects the eucharistic sacrifice and offers it to God in the name of all the people (No. 10).

The crucial amplification in this passage lies in what is said of the priest's sacred power who, once ordained with the Spirit of holiness, acts "in the person of Christ."

Dominicae Cenae explains this priestly power in an even more succinct way:

> The priest offers the holy sacrifice *in persona Christi*; this means more than offering 'in the name of' or 'in place of' Christ. *In persona* means in specific sacramental identification with 'the eternal high priest' (opening prayer, second votive Mass of the eucharist), who is the author and principal subject of this sacrifice of his, a sacrifice in which, in truth, no one can take his place. Only he—only Christ—was able and is always able to be the true and effective

[1] Vatican Council II, *Presbyterorum Ordinis*, 3, referring to Heb. 5:1.

'expiation for our sins and . . . for the sins of the world' (1 Jn. 2:2; cf. 4:10). Only his sacrifice—and no one else's—was able and is able to have a 'propitiatory power' before God, the Trinity, the transcendent holiness. Awareness of this reality throws a certain light on the character and significance of the priest celebrant who, by confecting the holy sacrifice and acting *in persona Christi*, is sacramentally (and ineffably) brought into the most profound sacredness and made part of it, spiritually linking with it in turn all those participating in the eucharistic assembly (No. 8).

In the eucharistic sacrifice, Christ himself acts through his priest. The priest, while remaining the same man, the same person, the same human being, is also at once identified with, even transformed into Christ, so that in the truest sense the priest may say, "This is my body"—because it is Christ who says it in him. One might also add that in exactly the same manner the priest absolves sins in the person of Christ in the sacrament of reconciliation, for the new covenant in the blood of Christ's sacrifice is given "so that sins may be forgiven."

Cardinal Joseph Ratzinger describes this sacramental identification in an interview published in his book *The Feast of Faith*:[2]

> You raised the question, 'Do we need a priest with the power to consecrate?' I would prefer not to speak of 'power,' although this term has been used since the early Middle Ages. I think it is better to approach it from another angle. In order that what happened then may become present now, the words 'This is my body—this is my blood,' must be said. But the speaker of these words is the 'I' of Jesus Christ. Only he can say them; they are his words. No man can dare to take to himself the 'I' and 'my' of Jesus Christ— and yet the words must be said if the saving mystery is not to remain something in the distant past. So authority is needed, and authority which no one can assume and which no

[2](San Francisco: Ignatius Press, 1986), p. 94.

congregation, nor even many congregations together, can confer. Only Jesus Christ himself, in the 'sacramental' form he has committed to the whole church, can give this authority. The word must be located, as it were, in sacrament; it must be part of the 'sacrament' of the church, partaking of an authority which she does not create, but only transmits. This is what is meant by 'ordination' and 'priesthood'.

Ordination is the focal point at which an authority possessed by Christ alone is transmitted to the priest: an authority to speak the "I" of Christ himself. Moreover, that authority involves a sacramental word. It involves an efficacy by which Christ renders the saving mystery of his once-for-all death present now so as to catch us up into his sacrifice. Thus, in virtue of his ordination the priest becomes the locus of that authority and efficacy in the eucharistic assembly—not by his own merits, not by any merely human activity of the church, but by the sacramental intervention of Christ.

Theologians sometimes speak of priestly ordination as conferring an "ontological" change on the ordinand—that is, a change in his very being. From what has been described above, one can see why they would consider such a change to be necessary. Only Christ and only his sacrifice could reconcile us to God; no other human or earthly efficacy could serve us. Therefore, in a priest appointed to renew that sacrifice in the person of Christ, a transition must occur from the unavailing level of the merely human to the efficacious level of Christ. This transition occurs thus in the ordination of a priest when through the laying on of hands and the invocation of the Spirit of holiness the bishop ordains a priest.

We are accustomed to thinking that such changes occur in the sacraments. In baptism, sinners are changed into the children of God. In the eucharist, bread is changed into the body of Christ. In both instances, we recall that the divine power which once created the universe is the same power at work in the sacraments. It is a power over being itself, summoning something from nothing, lovingly conserving and governing what it has summoned, transforming and reordering this still-incomplete universe until the whole of creation—physical, moral and spiritual—is ordered to the praise of God. Just as the sanctifying grace of our baptism enables us finite creatures to participate in the infinite life of the Trinity, so the grace of holy orders enables the priest, in all his weak humanity, to act in the incomparable person of Christ, the sinless, God-incarnate redeemer.

A. Task Orientation and Priestly Identity

In a practical, function-based, task-oriented society such as that of the contemporary West, it is easy to lose sight of this mystical reality at the heart of the ordained priesthood, easy even for priests themselves. Ours is a society obsessed with doing; questions of being seem remote to us. The liturgy, with its lofty unused spaces and its untroubled pace, seems an intrusion that must be made more serviceable. Even our leisure does not relax us, as we fill holidays with activity after activity and need a vacation to recover from vacation. If we lose sight of what the priest is, we focus instead on what he does. If we undervalue the liturgy and sacraments, then we may conclude that most of the priest's functions can be discharged by another just as well. And so the priesthood itself could seem an arbitrary and superfluous leftover from another time or culture.

Many philosophers, psychologists and social theorists have criticized this contemporary obsession with task and function. In various ways they have uncovered a profound restlessness and even sorrow at the root of our incessant activity: a lack of peace with the self, an inability to accept the self as a gift from God; an absence of the sense that this self is beloved of God and someone in whom he delights. Missing in our depths is an affirmation of our being. And, since no human being or human society can live without such affirmation, what results is a frantic drive to "earn" such affirmation through one's own efforts: through one's work, one's performance, one's own initiative. However, since none of these things can provide an affirmation that lasts and, rather than concluding to the futility of our effort, we step the process up, perpetuating the cycle.

Some even learn to prefer their work over their family or their community and cut themselves off from whatever chance of breaking the cycle.

Some have spoken of a "forgetfulness of being" as the contemporary crisis of the West: an obscuring mist spreading through Western spirit. Quaint as the expression sounds, we need to pay attention to it. For the current uneasiness of the West is not a diminution of physical existences or things; it is a subtle contraction of spirit, an impoverishment, a deeply felt (yet scarcely understood) loss—all while our daily life continues in its reassuring, nonchalant way.

The only remedy for the restlessness and sorrow at the root of our drivenness is a personal confidence and self-acceptance based on the love of God. We must learn to put our work into proper perspective. We must learn that God loves us no less on our day off—when we sleep late and putter around—than on our most productive work days. We must somehow recover prayer that sense of God's fatherhood over us. For just as a human father looks at his adult son and fondly remembers the little boy he still sees, so too as God looks on us he remembers that day without equal when he saw his reflection in the wet clay of the earth, picked it up, molded it, gave it the breath of life—and created man and woman. He was pleased then too because he saw that this creation was very good.

If we can recover such a sense, it will not be by simply adding another effort—now spiritual—to the many we already have. It will come, in part, only at right angles to the plane of our activity. It will come as a gift, a dispensation, a relaxation, even an interruption. And it will come in prayer. For this gift, this sense, this confidence, this self-acceptance together form part of a contemplative dimension for which we must make room in our lives. The priest as well must allow room for contemplation. He must set aside time, he must go off to a lonely place, in which he can allow himself to be touched by God's love. The constant exhortation of the church, the constant testimony of priestly experience, holds that prayer is essential to the nurturance of a priestly identity.

The priest himself first must appreciate the mystical character of the priestly office and appreciate the change of being that his ordination has brought about in him. The challenge of priestly spirituality is that, by God's grace, the priest realizes in his consciousness, in his deeds, indeed in his entire life the graced transformation that occurs because he acts in the person of Christ. In other words, his life is an effort to embody the holiness of Christ himself, especially in those moments when the priest celebrates the sacraments so that the people of God may truly see Christ in him and experience through him the care which Christ has for his church. In the rite of priestly ordination, the bishop presents the gifts of bread and wine to the newly ordained and tells him, "Imitate the mystery you celebrate." It is the whole pattern of the priest's conscious life. The medieval philosophers taught *agere sequitur esse*, "acting follows being." What we do follows from what we are. Or as St. Paul put it more pointedly, "Since we live by the spirit, let us follow the spirit's lead" (Gal. 5:25). When the life of the priest imitates the mystery which he celebrates, he becomes in the contemporary phrase "a man for others"—as Christ Jesus was for his Father and for us. Subsequently, everything the priest does, precisely as priest, derives from that reality.

The priest, of course, will be conscious of his sinfulness, of his unworthiness of the gift, of his many failures to respond adequately to the challenge of his state. This is why in the eucharist he prays privately before he receives communion. Like every other Christian, he must learn what it is to have faith in the love and mercy of Christ. For sinfulness has no more to say in one's receiving the gift of the priesthood than in one's receiving the life of grace itself. Both are Christ's gift, heedless of our merits. The Letter to the Hebrews, speaking of the high priesthood, reminds us, "No one takes this honor on himself, but only when called by God" (5:4). And Christ himself, in John's Gospel, tells us, "It was not you who chose me, it was I who chose you, to go forth and bear fruit, fruit that will last" (15:16). The preface of the Chrism Mass, as we have seen, celebrates the fact that Christ makes this choice "with a brother's love." For who knows failings better than a brother, only to love just the same?

Christ's commission to bear fruit is an important aspect of the priestly call. In the entirety of the Judeo-Christian tradition, divine election is always for the purpose of service of some sort. God's elective favor is not an end in itself. If the priest is a chosen one, he must also bear in mind that it belongs to the chosen in a particular way to realize the attitude of service, the servant humility and obedience of Christ.

B. The Mystical Meaning of Priestly Celibacy

Christ's commission to bear fruit has another meaning for the priest, since the priesthood of the Latin Catholic Church is exercised in celibacy, "at once a sign of pastoral charity and an incentive to it as well as . . . a source of spiritual fruitfulness in the world" (*Presbyterorum Ordinis*, 16). Just as it is necessary that the vine be pruned in order to increase its yield (Jn. 15:2), so the life of the celibate is, by the call of Christ, pruned of the ordinary attachments of family life, good as these are, in order to bring forth fruit of a different nature. As the Second Vatican Council taught:

> There are many ways in which celibacy is in harmony with the priesthood. For the whole mission of the priest is dedicated to the service of the new humanity which Christ, the victor over death, raises up in the world through his Spirit and which is born 'not of blood nor of the will of man, but of God' (Jn. 1:13). By preserving virginity or celibacy for the sake of the kingdom, priests are consecrated in a new and excellent way to Christ. They more readily cling to him with undivided heart and dedicate themselves more freely in him and through him to the service of God and of men. They are less encumbered in their service of his kingdom and of the task of heavenly regeneration. In this way they become better fitted for a broader acceptance of fatherhood in Christ (*Presbyterorum Ordinis*, 16).

Since Christ himself was unmarried, we may find it strange at first that the council speaks of fatherhood in Christ. Yet the hymn "*Summi Parentis Filio*" speaks of Christ as the father of the world to come. If we bear in mind what St. Paul teaches us about the spousal love of Christ for his church (see Eph. 5:22-33), we will see that this world to come is nothing less than the child of that union, the fruit of that love.

As celibacy is an imitation of Christ, it imitates too the union of Christ and the church. The council continues:

> By means of celibacy, then, priests ... recall that mystical marriage established by God and destined to be fully revealed in the future by which the church holds Christ as her only spouse. Moreover, they are made a sign of that world to come, already present through faith and charity, a world in which the children of the resurrection shall neither be married not take wives (*Presbyterorum Ordinis*, 16).

The priest, in union with Christ takes the church for his spouse to love, to cherish and to nurture. And from that union a true spiritual fatherhood ensues. It is not for nothing that the priest is addressed as "Father" by his people. As with the fatherhood of Christ, that of the priest points to the world to come; his solitude and earthly barrenness, a prefiguring of death; his prayer, pastoral charity and spiritual fruitfulness, a sign of God's power which is at work now to sanctify and so to yield eternal life.

On a number of occasions, most recently in his letter to priests on Holy Thursday, 1988, Pope John Paul II has spoken of the priesthood as a type of spiritual motherhood as well as fatherhood. By this image, he invokes the memory of St. Paul's Letter to the Galatians, in which the apostle compares his work with that church to the travail of childbirth (Gal. 4:19).

> Is not Paul's analogy on 'pain in childbirth' close to all of us in the many situations in which we too are involved in the spiritual process of man's 'generation' and 'regeneration' by the power of the Holy Spirit, the giver of life? The most powerful experiences in this sphere are had by confessors all over the world—and not by them alone.... Moreover, does not God himself, the creator and father, make the comparison between his love and the love of a human mother (cf. Is. 49:15; 66:13)? Thus we are speaking of a

characteristic of our priestly personality that expresses precisely apostolic maturity and spiritual 'fruitfulness' (No. 4).

In developing this image of motherhood for the priest, the Holy Father makes use of an extensive comparison with the Blessed Virgin Mary, whose motherhood is an instruction for the church as a whole and for the priest in particular. Just as she became a mother by faithfully welcoming the word of God, so must we. Just as she was given to the church at the foot of the cross when the disciple whom Jesus loved took her into his home, so must we take her into our hearts, especially we who are priests.

> Each of us, then, has to 'take her to our own home' like the apostle John on Golgotha; that is to say, each of us should allow Mary to dwell 'within the home' of our sacramental priesthood, as mother and mediatrix of that 'great mystery' (cf. Eph. 5:32) which we all wish to serve with our lives (ibid.).

In so welcoming her and thus in acknowledging a motherly dimension to our priesthood, we may expect to gain a more profound understanding of our celibacy, for the Virgin Mother has much to teach us about spiritual fruitfulness. The pope encourages us to place our choice of lifelong celibacy "within her heart" (ibid., 5), that heart which suffered alongside the divine Son at Golgotha as he consummated the salvation of the world. In welcoming her too, we may also expect to discover "in a new way the dignity and vocation of women, both in the church and in today's world" (ibid.).

Cardinal Jean-Marie Lustiger, the archbishop of Paris, in his book *Dare to Believe*,[3] describes ministerial celibacy as a "spiritual choice" of the Latin Catholic Church.

---

[3](New York: Crossroads, 1986).

A spiritual choice is achieved when an individual, a group or a church chooses to respond to the call of God, thus entering in a way of holiness and spiritual fruitfulness. What matters most at that moment is in no way the expected effectiveness nor the rational coherence of objectives with means, but the fulfillment of a divine will calling for an act of self-oblivion, self-surrender to the power of God. When Joan of Arc went to the stake, she made a spiritual choice and not a choice of political coherence or diplomatic effectiveness. When St. Vincent de Paul threw himself totally into the love of the poorest, he might certainly have answered economic needs, but in fact he responded to a spiritual choice. When the Western church made this spiritual choice, she was aware of obeying a call from God, and it is truly in such a way that all the reformers, the popes, the men of God, the spiritual people and popular consensus perceived priestly celibacy—as a demand of holiness, first of all and essentially a demand of holiness, whatever taboos or complexes might have been mixed with it (p. 204).

Thus the historical decision of the Latin Catholic Church in the Middle Ages to extend ministerial celibacy from the episcopate to the entire Western priesthood was not a practical matter, but rather a commitment to a certain type of ministerial holiness. In this commitment, both the church and the celibate priest freely surrender their freedom to God to allow the Holy Spirit to open a new path before them. The church subjects its own choosing of priests to the previous evidence that God has called certain men to the celibate vocation, and it freely restricts ordination to these alone. It is a choice with practical consequences:

The spiritual choice of the Western church is thus not to link priestly ordination with mere pastoral needs that could be tallied and projected by statistics. (This) enables us, paradoxically, to give way to a logic of gratuitousness, that is, of grace—since God does not reason in a technocratic way—to transform the number of ordinations from an administrative decision into a gift of faith" (p. 209).

The spiritual choice of the Roman Catholic Church has bracketed the question of an adequate ratio of priests to pastoral needs and has radically placed it in the hands of the provident God who leads us on our communal pilgrim path. Cardinal Lustiger explains in more detail:

> I cannot as a bishop say that for the good of my diocese, which has a certain number of communities and a certain population, I need a certain number of priests and that this need is a demand. Such reasoning would be a challenge to God. I can in the best of cases say this: There are many communities, and it would be good if we had that many priests. But I could not tell young men or a community that I demand so many priests. I can only pray with them that God awaken in the community enough generosity so that some will fully devote themselves to follow Christ (p. 207).

Thus the cardinal proposes an essentially spiritual approach to what is widely perceived as a crisis of numbers in the Roman Catholic priesthood. In effect, he suggests that seemingly practical needs are to be subjected "to the soverign freedom of the charisms and grace" (p. 206).

More to the point, he is clear-sighted about the element of risk involved in such a strategy:

> This then is a spiritual gamble for the church. How indeed are such charisms born? One could say that they come from the intertwining of human and divine freedom, but one can also say without falling into contradiction that they arise from the fervor inspired by the faith, hope and charity of a community, which thus becomes the ground for the charisms. In this view, we will say that the church bets that God does not cease to call men to make the spiritual offering of their whole life (p. 206).

It is a gamble for the church to set aside practical considerations and to give herself radically to the faith that God provides vocations to the celibate priesthood in sufficient numbers to meet contemporary pastoral needs. But as St. Paul told the Corinthians, "We walk by faith, not by sight" (2

Cor. 5:7). Faith itself is a gamble, at times a leap. If faith is strong, it can support the corporate risk of mandatory priestly celibacy, and it can do so in the spirit of trust and surrender to God's providence which that risk demands of both the community and the celibate. If faith is strong, it will inspire in the Catholic Church of northern Colorado the earnestness and fervor for the Gospel that can give rise in an individual to that at first audacious and awesome thought, Can God be calling me to the priesthood?

IV. Relating the Two Orders of Priestly Symbolism

To this point, we have examined the universal priesthood of the baptized and the distinction of the ordained priesthood within the church. Is it now possible to relate the two more clearly? For certainly, if the two are distinct, they nonetheless reflect the one priesthood of Christ Jesus, with its one mediating sacrifice. Perhaps it is best to look on the two orders of priestly symbolism in the church as two distinct ways of focusing on that single act of mediation. In the universal priesthood of the baptized, the focus is on the universal efficacy of Christ's mediation: on the fact that through the mediation of Christ all who belong to him indeed approach the Father (Heb. 7:23). In the ordained priesthood, the focus is on the unique mediator, Christ himself, the head of the body, the church: Christ as represented by the priest. Here the focus is on the fact that without Christ, we can do nothing (Jn. 15:5), on the fact that no one can come to the Father except through Christ (Jn. 14:6). But whether our focus is on the universal efficacy or the unique agent, the single reality we encounter is the one mediating act of Christ.

A. In the Eucharist

Beyond this consideration in principle, the clearest avenue for relating the two notions of priesthood lies in the eucharistic liturgy itself. Above all, it is in the eucharist that the two notions of priesthood come together. For in the eucharist, Christ is present in manifold ways. According to *Sacrosanctum*

Concilium, the Constitution on the Sacred Liturgy promulgated by the Second Vatican Council. Christ is present in his minister, he is present in the eucharistic species, he is present in the proclaimed word and he is present in the church that prays and sings (No. 7). Likewise, in *Lumen Gentium*, 10, the council taught that the two priesthoods are ordered to one another and share, each in its proper way, in the one priesthood of Christ. As such, in the eucharist the faithful "by virtue of their royal priesthood" offer their spiritual sacrifice, bringing forward their works, prayers, family life, leisure, hardships, their very selves as the gifts of bread and wine are presented at the altar.

Then, as we have seen in the words of *Dominicae Cenae*, the priest-celebrant, acting in the person of Christ and sacramentally united with the sacredness of his sacrifice, in turn unites to that sacrifice the lives and sacrifices of all those participating in the eucharist. As *Lumen Gentium* says of priests exercising their sacred functions in the eucharist:

> There, acting in the person of Christ and proclaiming his mystery, they united the votive offerings of the faithful to the sacrifice of Christ their head, and in the sacrifice of the Mass they make present again and apply until the coming of the Lord (cf. 1 Cor. 11:26), the unique sacrifice of the New Testament, that namely of Christ offering himself once for all a spotless victim to the Father (cf. Heb. 9:11-28) (No. 28).

The members of the universal priesthood offer his or her spiritual sacrifice in the eucharist. The ordained priest by virtue of his sacramental priesthood unites that sacrifice to the sacrifice of Christ, which he makes present.

This combination of priestly symbolisms may seem strange or even contradictory. One might respond, If we have a universal priesthood, then why an ordained priesthood? Or, If we have an ordained priesthood, is the universal priesthood anything more than window dressing? To answer these questions, we must remember that religion and the liturgy obey the rules not of logic, but of another realm—the realm of symbols.

For this realm usually combines symbols to reveal its secrets; it is untroubled by seemingly overlapping symbols and seldom sees contradiction where logic might readily do so. This is important to remember for other reasons as well.

It is, for instance, a characteristic of some communities of the Reformation to insist on disjunctive either-or solutions to complex religious realities. One of the strengths of the Roman Catholic Church is its sensitivity to the hidden laws governing the realm of symbols and its tolerance of the paradoxical tensions that result. Catholicism takes a characteristically both-and approach to the same complex realities others would simplify with recourse to the either-or solution. It does not choose between the universal priesthood and the ordained, it chooses both. The challenge of living in the resultant tension is to accept that we will never fully understand the reality we affirm—not, at least, to satisfy logic. But this unknowing is precisely what it means to live in the reality of mystery.

B. In the Life of the Priest

The two priesthoods also come together in the life of the priest himself. In its decree *Presbyterorum Ordinis*, the council observes that the priest, in addition to uniting the spiritual sacrifices of the people of God to the sacrifice of Christ, must also in that same act unite his own self-offering to that of the Lord (No. 13). Indeed, he makes that self-offering precisely by means of his whole ministry; he is "made strong in the life of the Spirit by exercising the ministration of the Spirit" (No. 12). He acquires personal holiness by exercising his priestly functions "sincerely and tirelessly in the Spirit of Christ" (No. 13). In particular, the council says:

> When priests unite themselves with the act of Christ the priest, they daily offer themselves completely to God, and by being nourished with Christ's body, they share in the charity of him who gives himself as food to the faithful (No. 13).

It was in fact in that sublime moment of self-giving on the

cross that Christ most fully manifested who he is: the eternal Son, lovingly come down from heaven "for us men and for our salvation" (Nicene Creed). He is the friend who gives his life for his friends in a love than which there is no greater (Jn 15:13). This is the divine charity in which priests partake when they give themselves wholly to their ministry: receiving gratefully for themselves and sharing generously with others.

In John 21:15-17, Jesus asks Peter three times, "Do you love me?" Three times, when Peter answers yes, Jesus gives him the care of the flock: "Feed my lambs.... Tend my sheep.... Feed my sheep." Perhaps a more apt Gospel description of the priestly ministry does not exist; for it is precisely in the work of "feeding" the flock, of caring for the faithful, that the priest, like the apostle Peter, expresses his own personal love of and commitment to Christ. Like each of the Twelve, with whose successors he is a co-worker, the priest is called by Jesus to be simultaneously a companion and an apostle: to be with Jesus and to be sent by him to preach the good news with spiritual power (see Mk. 3:14).

The spirituality and holiness of the priest is realized precisely through his priestly ministry and especially in the eucharist. The council earnestly recommended to the priest that he celebrate the eucharist daily, not only for the benefit to himself, but above all for the benefit of the church, since "in the mystery of the eucharistic sacrifice ... the work of our redemption is continually carried out" (*Presbyterorum Ordinis*, 13). The priest is sanctified by his service of the church, and to the extent that his service is a reflection of Christ, the church itself is sanctified as well—and this in a twofold sense. First, the church benefits from the work of the Redeemer, sacramentally rendered present through the ministry of the priest. But second, as the council teaches, "the very holiness of priests is of the greatest benefit for the faithful fulfillment of their ministry"; for God "prefers to show his wonders through those men who are ... submissive to the impulse and guidance of the Holy Spirit and who, because of their intimate union with Christ and their holiness of life, are able to say with St. Paul: 'It is no longer I who live but Christ who lives in me' (Gal 2:20)" (No. 12).

C. In the Cooperation of Pastors and Laity

A third manner in which the notions of the universal and ordained priesthood come together is in the increasingly common cooperation of pastors and laity in the work of the parish. The recent pronouncements of the Holy Father, Pope John Paul II, have reminded us of the doctrine of the Second Vatican Council that the primary lay apostolate is a secular one—in the world—namely, to order all of creation to the praise of God. The council envisioned this apostolate at work in our commerce and leisure and in the politics and culture of human society so as to transform society "as from within like leaven" (*Lumen Gentium*, 31). Nonetheless, the council also spoke of an exercise of the lay apostolate within the church. It is in this second exercise that we see yet another synthesis of the two orders of priestly symbolism.

In general according to the Second Vatican Council, the relation between pastors and the laity within the church should be a familiar one. Pastors are to recognize and promote the dignity, responsibility, zeal, initiative and liberty of the laity, allowing them scope for action. The laity are to disclose their needs with confidence to their pastors, accepting pastoral decisions "in Christian obedience" (*Lumen Gentium* 37). Likewise, they are to manifest their opinions in those matters for which they are particularly qualified to do so. Indeed, the council teaches that at times they are obliged to speak out for the good of the church, though prudently and through effective channels.

In September of 1987, during his visit to the United States, the Holy Father cautioned Catholics in America against two possible distortions of ministerial cooperation: the clericalization of the laity and the laicization of the clergy. In this, he simply insisted on the perspective of the Second Vatican Council. The lay apostolate is not meant to replace the clerical. Conversely, the clerical apostolate is principally a service within the church. The Holy Father has insisted, for example, that priests not campaign for or hold civil office, in part because the world of politics and civil government is a field of the lay apostolate.

In learning an appropriate cooperation between pastors and

laity, we must learn ever again the two-edged meaning of Paul's dictum, "There are a variety of gifts but one Spirit" (1 Cor. 12:4). Certainly there are more gifts than simply the ordained ministry in the church; there are many gifts—all ordered to the benefit of the whole. But neither do the many gifts obviate the church's eternal need for the unique gift of the apostles, first in rank among the gifts and likewise given for the benefit of the whole. Discord and contentiousness show an absence of the Spirit, a failure to have learned the shared responsibility to which the Spirit is leading us. The Gospels are throughout a lesson in an ecclesiology of service and never more so than when speaking of authority. The followers of Christ do not exercise authority in the manner of princes, but as Christ did, who came "not to be served by others, but to serve, to give his own life as a ransom for the many" (Mt. 20:28). Where this lesson is learned, the church's ministry is rendered more effective by the complementarity of gifts and by the mutual support of pastors and laity. The fruits of the Spirit will be abundant.

Conclusion

I opened these reflections with a prayer for wisdom of heart concerning the mystery of priestly consecration, a prayer which is all the more necessary because wisdom is a divine gift. In concluding, I want to make some recommendations concerning that prayer.

First, we need as a church to deepen our personal faith in the power of the Spirit in the consecration of priests: that Spirit of holiness sent by the Father, who is the source of every honor and dignity. We need to ask in prayer for his deepening of faith, since faith too is a divine gift. Moreover, we need to open ourselves to receive that gift; perhaps we even need to seek that openness in prayer. Wisdom is the daughter of faith, and we who desire any measure of understanding of the mystery of the priesthood must, in St. Augustine's classic formula, first believe in order to understand.

Then we need to ask for the gift of understanding, that

perfection of the gift of faith by which the Holy Spirit himself moves our mind to an intuitive penetration of revealed truth. I have shown already that in the hierarchical ministry the church possesses an essential element of the mystery of its life in Christ Jesus. Through the gift of faith, God enables us to live that mystery in all its aspects; through the gift of understanding, he enables us to have some sense of what that living means, even if we can never fully articulate that sense. Together, these two gifts establish in the church a sense of sympathy for the mystery of God's purpose—a sympathy that supplies at least patience for the halting way in which that mystery is lived and expressed by weak human beings in the church.

I want to recommend this prayer especially to priests and to priesthood candidates. For priests the need of these gifts of faith and understanding is an ongoing one, since their personal identity now in some sense, by the grace of God, incorporates the mystery of the priesthood. As I have said earlier, prayer is essential to the nurturance of a priestly identity, with its sacramental link to the sacrifice of Christ. Moreover, since the gift of faith alone gives meaning to the spiritual choice of celibacy, we priests must pray for that faith, to live that choice with a full heart.

In connection with this call for prayer, I wish to add a further recommendation to the priests of the archdiocese: that every rectory contain an oratory with the eucharist reserved to facilitate this prayer of priests individually and together, and to demonstrate the essential, dynamic relationship between the priesthood and the eucharist.

As I bring these reflections to a close, two images are uppermost in mind. One is the magnificent vision of the Second Vatican Council, described in *Sacrosanctum Concilium* (No. 41) and the General Instruction of the Roman Missal (No. 74), a vision which the council itself borrowed from St. Ignatius of Antioch: that celebration of the eucharist at which the bishop presides, surrounded by his deacons and ministers and by the college of his presbyters, and in which the people of God take a full and active part. This celebration, as both texts state, is the principal symbol in which the church

manifests the mystery of what it is. In this celebration we see
both the hierarchical diversity of ministries and their ordering
to one another for the unity of the church.

More to the point in that ordering, that is, in a mutual
submission of one Christian to another in charity and in
service, the church shows forth most fully the image of the
Master, "who loves us and freed us from our sins by his own
blood, who has made us a royal nation of priests in the service
of his God and Father"(Rv. 1:5-6). The culminating realization
of that image is the Chrism Mass of Holy Week, when the
assembled church at once celebrates the priesthood, blesses the
healing balm which the priest administers and reenacts the
source of all ecclesial and sacramental life in the paschal
mystery. May that liturgy hold for us the importance which it
deserves.

The second image is an image of ministry within that grace-
filled assembly: The image of Jesus rising from the table at the
Last Supper, putting aside his outer garment, putting on an
apron and washing the feet of his apostles (see Jn. 13:1-17).
Let all Christians, especially priests, bear that image in mind
as they begin the eucharist. If Jesus, whom we address as
teacher and Lord, could humble himself to wash our feet, then
we must do the same for one another. In part, it is a shocking
image, and Peter's protest anticipates our own; but it is a
deeply affecting image, for each of us recognizes the truth of
Jesus' reply to Peter: We must allow him to serve us. We
simply do not have the wherewithal to attain on our own a
share in his divine life. As ministers, let us allow the image to
speak from within us, wordlessly and without self-conscious-
ness. "Let us love in deed and truth and not merely talk about
it" (1 Jn. 3:18).

The Sacramental Identity of the Ministerial Priesthood[1]

Daniel M. Buechlein, O.S.B.
Bishop of Memphis

Introduction: Ministry at the Crossroads

The proper context for understanding the ministerial priesthood is the mystery of the Church. And of course the starting point for understanding the mystery of the Church is the incarnation of Jesus Christ.

A vision of Church is necessarily sacramental. Preeminently the eucharist maintains the Christic center of the Church's lived experience as the Body of Christ.

The Church, divinely instituted, is a communitarian structure of salvation for the human family. It is a body, an assembly, a community.

The Church as a community has a ministry and a mission which is eschatological. It is to proclaim the gospel to the outer limits of the world. The Church is ministerial or missionary.

George Tavard beautifully summarizes this thought: "There is an identity in mystery between Church and eucharist. The identity is between *Christ given for us*, the *eucharist* in which we receive *Christ given for us*, the *ecclesia* into which we are

---

[1] This paper is taken from a series of lectures given as part of a course on Priestly Ministry and Spirituality at Saint Meinrad Seminary in 1986.

built by *Christ given for us*, and the mission of the kingdom in which we expect and announce the return of *Christ given for us.*"[2]

The identity of the ministerial priesthood is necessarily Christological. Christ is, after all, *the* Word and *the* gesture of eternal salvation. Christ is the sacrament of eternal salvation, and in these "last days," the Church is the primordial sacrament of Christ. The sacraments of the Church are the particular way in which the Church is the primordial sacrament of eternal salvation—the way the Church is "the means" to salvation.

One can say the sacraments of the Church are intended to be effective symbols and rituals of the ways in which the community of the Church and the Lord himself "walk with" individual members of the Body of Christ through the cross-roads of life. Birth, growing up, beginning a new state of life, illness and death are liminal or "crossing over" experiences of life. "Crossing over" or liminal experiences are times one feels alone. No one is born for me, no one chooses and accepts my state of life for me, no one can take my sickness from me, no one dies for me. These are key *kairos* and *chronos* "moments" of life which are lonesome and for which one needs community support.

The Christian community, the Church by divine institution, has ritualized these moments with seven sacraments. In symbolic sacramental ritual the Church offers community support for the liminal or crossing-over experiences from the very beginning of life until its ending. By divine institution, the ministry of the Twelve handed on by apostolic succession provides the sacramental ministry of the Church.

Because of the priestly ministry of the Church, one need not face the crossroads of life alone. Indeed, one can say that as a designated leader and also representative of community, the priest is called and ordained to live at the crossroads of life. Of its very nature, the ministerial priesthood suggests a way of life that walks with the human family and its individual members through every crossing over that happens in life, even death

[2]George H. Tavard, *A Theology For Ministry,* Theology and Life Series, 6, p. 54.

itself. Priestly ministry, sacramental ministry in its *strict* and in its *broadest* sense, is radically liminal. The sacramental minister lives at the crossroads of life and he can help others negotiate *their* crossroads, because as the leader and designated representative of the community, and the Lord, he lives there. The crossroads are the home of sacramental ministers; and from this vantage point the priest helps others to find the right path to their home, which isn't at the crossroads.

And if in this imagery of crossroads and liminality one detects an eschatological note about life at the crossroads, that's on the mark. A lot of what is negotiated at all stages of life is a constant call to crossover, to turn to the kingdom which is begun but not yet fulfilled.

The life of Jesus was and is the quintessential life at the crossroads. He is in fact the only way of crossing over. But ministry in the name of Jesus is more than professional management of life at confusing intersections. It is also more than orchestrating worship services or leading the community in ritual. "Standing in" for the person of Jesus and for the community at the crossroads makes demands on the very being of the minister and it affects every aspect of his daily life. The choice of a liminal life, living on the margin, living at the crossroads is the choice of the emptying life of Jesus. It is an identification with the *kenosis* of his life. One might say priests are to be icons of the self-emptying Jesus at the crossroads of life, *for* the community and *in the name of* the community.

The Mystery of the Priesthood in the Mystery of the Church [3]

The mystery of the Catholic priesthood is rooted in the mystery of the Church. Only within a theology of sign, a theology which explicitly considers the Church as the sacra-

---

[3]Much of the theme of this paper is borrowed from a wonderful little study by Jean M.R. Tillard, O.P., "The Ordained 'Ministry' and the 'Priesthood' of Christ," *One in Christ* 14 (1978), pp. 231-246. The article first appeared in *Irenikon*, no. 2, 1976, pp. 147-66.

ment of the risen body of the Lord, the High Priest, is there
hope for a full understanding of who priests are.

God chose a moment and a place in the human world and
he sent his Son into the universe to bring grace and mercy in
human word and in human gesture. This *is* sacrament. Christ
is *the* sacrament; he is *the* visible Word and gesture. He *is*
salvation made visible in our history.

The words and gestures of Jesus were not mere show or
"play acting" about salvation. The word and action of Jesus
were at one and the same time grace and sign of grace; they
were salvation in visible form. Jesus is the effective sacrament
of our salvation.

No one except Jesus has, by right and in fact, entered God's
own sanctuary, the place of radical nearness to and intimacy
with God. Nor has any one except Jesus been once-for-all
immolated as the sacrifice which totally belongs to God. And
no one except Jesus has entered the heavenly sanctuary to
present his own blood in an unrepeatable sacrifice which totally
returns to God what is his. Perfect victim and perfect minister
of the altar are joined in the fullness of priesthood. In the very
act of going to the Father with his whole life, Jesus is "consecrated" and set apart as the priest. The consecration of Christ
in the unique fullness of priesthood was achieved in the
wonderful mystery of his death, resurrection and ascension.

But what about now? Jesus is no longer visible to us in his
human body. Unless the salvation intended for us is for
nothing, once Jesus returned to the sanctuary of the Father as
eternal High Priest, then Jesus, the sacrament of salvation,
must be available to us in some form we can see and experience.

The Church declares explicitly that she is the sacrament of
Christ, that she is the active presence of Christ in time and
place, visible to all. The very meaning of the Church is caught
up in the activity of God calling a people in space and time. (It
is the continuation of Salvation History.)

It was the mission of Jesus Christ to draw people to visible
union with him and each other in his mystical body which we
call the Church. As High Priest, and Head of the Body, Jesus
continues to exercise the leadership role in the Church today.

His call to union with him and with each other is the call to salvation. Communion is the very purpose of the perfect sacrifice which he offers on the altar of the heavenly sanctuary.

It is in his role as head of the body and as High Priest that Jesus calls all members to unity in his Body. Jesus Christ as High Priest and Head of the Body draws all people to saving community, the fruit of his perfect offering. The Church is the sacrament, the visible sign and the reality *of this unifying activity of Christ.*

The Church is also the visible sign and the reality of the Christian community's activity *of being united in Christ.* The Church is both the sacrament of Jesus calling *and* the sacrament of a community, a Body called.

The Fathers of Vatican Council II describe the "corporate Christ" like this: "The Head of this Body is Christ. He is the image of the invisible God and in Him all things came into being. He is before all creatures and in Him all things hold together. He is the Head of the Body which is the Church."[4]

But if the whole Christ is head and members, then the sacrament of the risen Christ must visibly be both head and members. If the risen Christ is head and members, the sacrament of the risen Christ must visibly be both head and members. if he is High Priest, he must visibly be so now.

Vatican Council II states that those who participate in the sacrament of orders are representative of Christ in his leadership role as head of the Church and as High Priest. The *Constitution on the Sacred Liturgy* says the celebrant at eucharist is to be one "who presides over the assembly in the person of Christ."[5] The *Decree on Priestly Life and Ministry* reads: "The sacerdotal office of priests is conferred by that special sacrament through which priests, by the anointing of the Holy Spirit, are marked with a special character and are so configured to Christ the Priest that they can act in the person of Christ the Head."[6]

---

[4]Dogmatic Constitution on the Church, (*Lumen Gentium*), No. 7.

[5]Constitution on the Sacred Liturgy, (*Sacrosanctum Concilium*), No. 33.

[6]Decree on the Ministry and Life of Priests, (*Presbyterorum Ordinis*), No. 2.

Ministerial priesthood is the visible presence of Christ as he calls all people to unity. Ministerial priesthood is a sacrament for the unity of the Church. Ministerial priesthood is a sacrament of Christ the pastoral leader, the pastor. The ministerial priesthood is the visible presence of Christ the High Priest. It is the sacrament of Christ as Head of the Body and as High Priest.

Who are priests? Priests are sacraments. To use another image, priests are icons of the pastoral leadership of the One who calls the people of God to unity and priests are the visible icon of the priesthood of Jesus.[7]

Who are priests? The ministerial priesthood is the sacrament of the headship, the pastoral leadership (of Jesus) and it is the sacrament of the priesthood of Jesus.

The grace to be a sacrament of the unifying leadership of Christ and of his unique priestly role is given in ordination. In virtue of this sacramental reality, the priest has the power to preside in the person of Christ at the eucharist; it is in virtue of the sacramentality of the headship of Christ the High Priest, that the priest has the power to absolve sins and to be the instrument of paschal reconciliation. In his role as sacrament of the pastoral leadership of Jesus, the priest is authorized by the Church and ultimately by God, to proclaim the Lord's call to unity; and the priest is authorized to draw together all those who, by their baptism, exercise another form of priesthood which is membership in the whole Body called to worship the Father in spirit and in truth.

The ministerial priest calls sisters and brothers to the priesthood of a holy life in the *ecclesia,* the assembled community of faith and to participate in the mission of salvation.

Just as the entire community is most visibly the Body of Christ, i.e. most visibly Church, when it is gathered around the table of the Lord both to hear the Lord's Word and to be fed by his body, (and thus to worship the Father in spirit and in truth,) so the priest is most visibly the sacrament of Christ the Head and Christ the Priest when he presides at the table of the

---

[7]The image of "icon" is used by J.M. Tillard, O.P., op.cit., p. 240.

Lord. Priests are most visibly who they are in the community at the table of the Lord—at the breaking of the bread.

The Church can be fully present as head and members of Christ at eucharist only where there is an honest community of priests and lay people, sharing their faith and their struggle and, above all, sharing their love in ministry.

In relationship to other Christians who rightfully claim their part in the worship and unifying service of the Church, priests are to be leaders and signs of the unifying activity of Jesus. To claim such leadership takes the understanding, courage and the humility to be no more (and no less) than authentically designated leaders in the manner of him who came to serve.

Dominican scholar, J.M.R. Tillard, uses the Eastern image of "icon" to picture who priests are to be; icons are not just "flat" pictures. They are images which somehow contain the very mystery they represent. Priests are icons of Jesus, as the one who serves unity and icons of Jesus as the one and only High Priest.

There are other icons of Jesus. Can we not say that the poor, the suffering, the oppressed are icons of Jesus, *the victim*? Can we not see the face of Jesus in every sister and brother, all of whom together are icons of the holiness of Jesus who leads us in worship "in spirit and in truth?"

Yet it is distinctive and essentially different to be the icon of Jesus as one who calls to unity, (pastoral leadership), and an icon of Jesus as High Priest, the one who offers his very own blood that has saved us all. The distinction is to serve communion, not division in the Church.

Ordination: Configuration to Christ by the Spirit

By anointing and consecration at baptism, all people are joined to Christ in worship of the Father and in service of his Body. We are initiated, if you will, into the priesthood of a holy life.

The ministerial priesthood participates in the High Priesthood of Jesus in the sense that it serves the once-for-all sacrifice of Christ by making it visibly present in the community of believers. The ministerial priesthood becomes the *means* or the *channel* through which the priesthood of the holy life can be realized in the Church. Ordained priests are called to serve the bond between Christ the High Priest and the community of believers who are the Body.

Priests are not only *icons* of Jesus the Priest and pastoral leader, they are also the *doulos*, the servant of the one priesthood.[8]

Just as they are able to participate in the priesthood of a holy life through the gift of the Spirit received in baptismal consecration, so it is by the gift of the same Spirit received in the consecration of orders that priests are put at the service of the priesthood of Jesus. By ordination, priests are *enabled* to serve the priesthood of Jesus by sharing *the very same Spirit* in whom Jesus accomplished his priestly ministry.

Far from being used as mere mechanical instruments, far from being mere blurred photographs of Jesus as High Priest and Head of the Body, "the Spirit wills to draw us into a communion *of behaviour* with the One we serve."[9]

Tillard says so beautifully: "At ordination the Spirit wants to unite us as closely as possible with what lay at the heart of the priesthood of Jesus: his gift of all of himself for those who belonged to him."[10] The self-emptying gift of his very self, the gift and his death are nothing but the manifestation of who Jesus is at the deepest level of his being, as the one who comes from God and goes to God.

Consecration by the very same Spirit to service of the priesthood of Jesus, therefore, is also to be a service of one's entire life, not just a service of some functions or tasks. Participation in the priesthood of Jesus by the grace of holy orders must be understood as communion in the Spirit with the priesthood of Jesus. Hence communion with the self-emptying Jesus is part of the charism of orders. Communion through the Spirit with Jesus and generous service go together.

---

[8] Cf. Tillard, op.cit., p. 238.

[9] Cf. Tillard, ibid.

[10] Ibid.

Herein lies the key to understanding the permanence of commitment in the ministerial priesthood. Herein lies the key to understanding the ontological nature of the priest's relationship to Jesus the Priest. Herein is the key to understanding the call to live one's entire priestly life in the simple way in which Jesus lived.

Communion in the Spirit with Jesus is effected by sacramental anointing and consecration. Herein lies the key to understanding why accepting the call to ministerial priesthood is more than accepting a different "lifestyle." Unless one's life is to be a mere *lifeless* echo of what others say about the Word of God and a lifeless drama of sacramental ministry, one's own *experience* of *communion with Jesus* must be *joined* to priestly service.

The Catholic doctrine about the grace of the sacrament of holy orders is based on the relation of the person of the priest with Christ the pastoral priest. The presence of Christ as pastoral priest in the midst of his people is made visible through the sacramentality of the ministerial priesthood. Priests are called to be icons of Christ in the most dynamic sense. Authenticity means communion with the mystery of Jesus.

Now, the Holy Spirit acts through priests for the good of the Church even when they are personally unworthy—that is the point of affirming a priestly "character," a power to act in Christ's name in the sacramental forum even when they are personally unworthy. But when that is true, when priests are not trying to be who they say they are and appear to be, then the People of God do not have an authentic image or icon of Christ the Priest and Christ the Pastor.

When priests are blurred in their very lives in ministry, then the Body of Jesus is truly wounded. The blind and the lame and the deaf are left with a lifeless echo. And what about the priest? Being a "lifeless echo" is a miserable kind of emptiness— not the self-emptying love of Jesus. And so it is so important that the very depth of one's life as a priest be confronted totally by his relationship to Jesus who is the Word of God.

The ministerial priest is not only *doulos*, servant, to the headship and priesthood of Jesus. The priest is also servant to the community which calls him to that sacramental role within its midst. The sacramental service of the ministerial priesthood belongs to the community, to the whole body—and not vice versa.

Viewing the ministerial priesthood as the sacrament of Jesus the Pastor and Jesus the Priest within the Body of the Church is an effective way to understand the distinctive role of the ministerial priest. Based on the human reality, Jesus who is the sacrament of eternal salvation must be visible somehow. Granted that he is visible through the Body of the Church, it is also necessary that he somehow be visibly present distinctively as Head of the Body and as High Priest within the body. The ministerial priesthood is the sacrament of Jesus as pastor and priest, i.e. as Head of the Body.

One can see that the acceptance and living of that role, which can be accomplished only by the grace of consecration in the Spirit, makes an *existential claim* on the very person of the priest. True, the effectiveness of the sacramental ministry being done in the name of Jesus, the objective power of grace is there no matter what quality of ministry is given. Still the self-emptying disposition of the minister is part and parcel of being sacrament of the self-emptying leadership for unity and the priestly act of Jesus. The very person and disposition of the servant to the priesthood of Jesus and to the community as well, *definitely affects* the faith of the Christian community.

Hence priestly ministry is not merely a career or part-time profession. It is a great deal more than living a "style" of life. The icon imagery works very well here. In the culture and mentality of the orient, there is an enormous difference between a photo and an icon. There is the sense that in an icon there is more than simply the pictorial presence.

The vision of ministerial priesthood as a sacrament of Jesus, pastor and priest, allows for elaboration of other dimensions of priestly ministry which are present by implication. Certainly the role of Jesus the Teacher is implicit in his headship of the body. In fact the entire development of this paper would easily allow for the traditional interpretation of Christ as Priest, Prophet and King.

Appendix
A Message on the Priesthood
William Cardinal Baum

This appendix by William Cardinal Baum, prefect of the Vatican's Congregation for Seminaries and Educational Institutions, contains the highlights of a report which summarizes a five-year Apostolic Visitation of American Seminaries. The address was presented on September 28, 1988, at the Pontifical College Josephinum in Columbus, Ohio.

When John Paul II became Pope, he introduced a new sort of Apostolic Visitation emphasizing that the successors to the apostles, the bishops, acting in union with the Bishop of Rome, conduct a review of the state of some aspect of the life of the Church. In the case of priestly formation, the Holy Father has asked for these Visitations to "take the pulse" of the seminaries to see how well they are doing, to assess how securely Vatican II has been implemented in them.

In 1981, Pope John Paul II asked for a Visitation of all the seminaries in the United States. Following a suggestion of the Episcopal Conference the Congregation for Catholic Education—now known as the Congregation for Seminaries and Educational Institutions—formally nominated Bishop John Marshall of Burlington, Vermont, as the apostolic visitor.

Bishop Marshall immediately set out to consult the interested parties and to prepare an "instrument" for the Visitation. He also recruited about 70 bishops, religious superiors and experienced seminary administrators and professors to assist in the work of the Visitation.

These were divided into teams, usually of five or six members, with the various responsibilities divided among them—administration, faculty, admissions, academics, spiritual and liturgical formation, formation for celibacy, apostolic or pastoral formation, evaluations, community life and discipline, etc. Monsignor Donald Wuerl acted as secretary, and later

Monsignor Richard Pates took over from him. Their contribution has been invaluable.

After two years of consultation and preparation, the actual Visitations began. These were programmed to take place twice a year in late winter and early fall, usually with ten or a dozen Visitations all taking place at the same time. Six months before a Visitation was scheduled, each seminary sent to Bishop Marshall a self-examination and a complete set of the seminary's documentation, covering every possible aspect of its program. Bishop Marshall shared this documentation with the members of the team who were to make the actual Visitation.

When the team arrived at the seminary, they spent a week interviewing the rector, the faculty, the staff, a good number of the students, bishops who sponsor the students, a sampling of pastoral supervisors, priests ordained during the last five years, and others they thought might be profitably interviewed. On the last day of the Visitation, the rector and the Ordinary were given a verbal report on the team's findings. Often the whole faculty was present for this report.

The team then went away, and each member put into writing his part of the report. These parts were collated and sent to Bishop Marshall who put them into a standard format and forwarded them through the Apostolic Nunciature in Washington to the Congregation for Catholic Education in the Vatican. Each Ordinary and rector was shown the written report before it was sent to Rome so that they knew in justice what was being said of their seminary, although the report at this stage was only provisional.

Each provisional report was analyzed in Rome, and on the basis of that analysis a letter was sent by the Congregation to the Ordinary concerned. This letter is THE report, and it expresses the mind of the Holy See about the state of the seminary and the quality of its priestly formation program. It usually contains both commendations and recommendations. Each Ordinary is expected to report back to the Congregation one year after receiving the report to describe what progress has been made in implementing the recommendations.

Each year, Bishop Marshall has been received in audience

by the Holy Father to discuss the progress of the Visitation. The Apostolic Visitation has been conducted in 221 centers of priestly formation in the United States, including diocesan and religious theologates and colleges, schools of theology and houses of formation. The American colleges in Louvain and in Rome have also been part of the Visitation.

I would say the most important matter to have been brought to light by the Visitation is the question: *What IS the priesthood?* What does this seminary think the priesthood is? Is this seminary's understanding of the priesthood *sound, theologically informed, in accordance with the teaching of the Magisterium of the church?*

We are not asking each seminary to work out its own model of the priesthood on a sort of do-it-yourself basis. We are not asking each seminarian to formulate his own theology of the priesthood out of his own creativity and subjectivity. We are asking each seminary and each seminarian to bring out clearly *the Church's understanding of the priesthood.* "In many and in various ways God spoke of old to our fathers by the prophets; but in these last days he has spoken to us by a Son, whom he appointed heir of all things, through whom he also created the world" (Heb 1:1-2).

God has made his Revelation in history. That Revelation in word and deed is entrusted to the Church so that it be handed on in its integrity to each generation, maintaining its identity through the centuries. The unity of the Sacred Scriptures, of Tradition and of the teaching office of the Church was brought out clearly by Vatican Council II in the Constitution *Dei Verbum,* for "they are so linked and joined together that one cannot stand without the other" (n. 10).

This fundamental truth must be always followed in our exegesis and use of Holy Scripture, in our study and analysis of the historical data of the Apostolic Age and in our theological reflection on the ordained priesthood.

The priesthood is part of the Revelation of God; the establishment of what we term Holy Orders by Our Lord is clear; for he called the Twelve, he instructed them and formed them, charging them with a ministry to exercise and to hand on. Within the New Creation of the Church, Our Lord established a special group of ministers. As the years went by, the shape of that ministry clearly emerged; and although there are still many details of that historical process to be researched, the central fact of an ordained, hierarchical ministry is plain; and it emerged as tri-partite: bishops, priests and deacons.

Within the new People of God there are some who are set apart for special priestly service. This is writ large on the pages of the New Testament. It is the principle underlying the Epistle of Clement to the Corinthians. It is the doctrine expounded by Ignatius of Antioch in his letters to the churches. It is doctrine found and promoted in the writings of the Fathers of the Church both in the East and in the West.

An understanding of the duties of the priest—the practical job description—is not enough. An understanding of the theology of the priesthood is essential. The teaching of the 23rd session of the Council of Trent on the doctrine of holy orders said a character is imprinted in the sacrament of orders as it also is imprinted in baptism and confirmation, that theological tradition was expressed anew and emphatically by the Second Vatican Council in its Decree on the Priesthood, *Presbyterorum Ordinis* (n. 2). In *Lumen Gentium*, the Council Fathers noted that the common priesthood of all the faithful and the ordained priesthood differ from one another "in essence and not only in degree" (n. 10).

These are very important matters, and the student for the priesthood needs to be well grounded in them. He also needs to know the theological basis for the relationship between priest and bishop, since an understanding of their sacramental order will foster an effective pastoral cooperation and unity, for "Bishops enjoy the fullness of the sacrament of orders, and all priests as well as deacons are dependent upon them in the exercise of authority" (*Christus Dominus*, n. 15).

The seminaries in the United States that are the most successful are those that hand on to their students a clear idea of the priesthood thoroughly grounded in theology and in wholehearted fidelity to the Magisterium.

In doing this, the successful seminary has to meet and surmount a number of hurdles, or issues: phenomena within the Church of our day. It meets these issues openly, and in bringing out the distinctive character of the ordained priesthood in relation to them is, in its turn, enriched by them. I refer to the rather generalized *concept of ministry*, the renewed emphasis on the *common priesthood of all the faithful*, the crisis of confidence in *priestly celibacy*, and the influence of pressure emanating from the movement for the *ordination of women*. I wish to comment on each of these in turn.

Firstly, the *concept of ministry*. In recent years we have become much more aware of the variety of "ministries" in the Church. "Ministry" is not restricted to those in holy orders. The Church has introduced the lay ministries of lector and acolyte, but the language of ministry has developed, replacing the old terminology of the "lay apostolate" and is now often used to describe, sometimes without precision, the whole range of Christian service and Catholic organization.

We must differentiate between the various ministries in the Church, and while our seminarians gain an insight into the necessity and value of ministry rendered by lay people and religious, they must have a clear understanding of the ministry of the ordained priest—in Word and Sacrament, in community leadership and in pastoral care.

Secondly, the distinction between the ministry of the priest and the ministry of others depends, of course, on a theological distinction needed because of renewed emphasis on the *common priesthood of all the faithful*. When we are baptized we become members of a priestly people. Perhaps the simplest way to understand this is to think of the Catholic community at Mass. Since offering sacrifice is a priestly task, the community which offers the sacrifice of the Mass is a priestly community. But we must not confuse this concept of priesthood with the ordained priesthood. The priestly people that assembles on a Sunday cannot offer the Sacrifice without an ordained priest to lead them, to exercise the Ministry of the Word with authority, especially in his preaching, to invoke the Holy Spirit and bring about the real presence of Our Lord by changing the bread and wine into his Body and Blood.

There is only one High Priest, Jesus Christ Our Lord himself, and there is only one priesthood, that of Jesus Christ, the word Incarnate. He shares his priesthood with us in a general way in baptism and confirmation, and in a special distinctive way in orders. He is prophet, priest and king. All members of his Body, the Church, share in these offices, but the sharing made possible by baptism and confirmation is not the same as the sharing into which the ordained priest is initiated. Our seminarians need to know the theology of the common priesthood, and the theology of the ordained priesthood, understanding the relationship between them, their mutuality and their differences.

It is not only what a priest *does* which distinguishes his ministry; it is also what he *is*. When a priest is ordained, his very being is marked in some way; changed, made different. This is not for his sake, for his honor or to his own personal credit. It is for the sake of the Church. As a seminarian prepares to share through the sacrament of holy orders in the ministry of the Good Shepherd, Prophet, Priest and King, he needs to have a thorough understanding of what happens to him in ordination.

This sort of phenomenon underlines once more the need for study of the priesthood in preparation for ordination. Some provide it in short courses as the students get ready for candidacy, for the office of lector, acolyte, diaconate and priesthood. Others provide it by extending the course on the sacramental theology of orders. Others introduce a special course at the beginning of the seminary program.

Thirdly, I want to say something about the *celibacy of priests* in the Western Latin tradition, though I fully respect the tradition of the eastern churches. Our Lord's whole life was sacrifical. He gave up his own life—in obedience to his Father's will—in order to serve others. The fulfillment of his sacrificial life was his Passion and Death. But there is another aspect of Our Lord's sacrificial life which is very important: he was celibate. In the Roman Catholic Church we ask our priests to be celibate. In fact, it is a condition of ordination. We expect our priests to pattern in their lives as closely as possible the sacrifical life of Our Lord, his loving care for the people, and a total obedience to the Father.

But celibacy is under attack. Sadly, many priests have left the priesthood. They have preferred to marry. Many people say that celibacy does not work, that it is too difficult, that it is not natural, and that it is not reasonable of us to require that our priests be celibate. Then, there have been failures on the part of some priests, and each one of these failures is used to undermine the credibility of celibacy. Indeed, some point to these failures precisely to attack celibacy. Some people want to see married priests.

For particular reasons we have sometimes ordained married converts to the Roman Catholic Church, but in every case these men were formerly ordained ministers of one or another Christian communion. These cases are few and rare. They are not the thin end of the wedge, preparing the Western Church for married priests in general.

The fourth issue that tests a seminary's understanding of the priesthood comes from the movement for the *ordination of women*. The ordained priesthood is reserved to men. This does not mean that men are better than women. It means that when the Second Person of the Trinity became flesh, he took the male form of being human. He chose men to be his apostles, and the Church has continued to ordain only men to stand at the alter *in persona Christi*. This is the tradition of the Church both in the East and in the West. This is the teaching of the Church.

In our modern world there is some confusion about masculinity and femininity; and motherhood and fatherhood are neglected and undervalued. We need to maintain a proper communion, partnership and complementarity between motherhood and fatherhood in the family, and between men and women in the life and service of the Church. In fact, we have been blessed in recent years by a real flowering in the Church of lay involvement by men and women across the continents.

When a seminary has a clear, authentic understanding of the priesthood, its enterprise of priestly formation is correctly focused. This leads to the building of a program that is systematic and balanced between the spiritual and liturgical, the academic and the apostolic and pastoral. The academic dimension becomes more substantial the more the priesthood is understood. I would go so far as to say: vague, confused idea of the priesthood—vague, confused curriculum: clear, authentic idea of the priesthood—clear, profound curriculum: knowledge of and confidence in Vatican II's agenda for priestly formation—confidence in and vigor of the seminary enterprise as a whole.

I have mentioned these *four issues* because of their contemporary importance. There is a whole range of priestly formation topics, though, which are fundamental, and which we have treated at length in our general letters on the theologates and the colleges. I refer to the spiritual and liturgical dimensions of formation, to ecumenism, to what we call apostolic formation in the colleges and pastoral formation in the theologates. In all these dimensions the primacy of holiness is paramount. I do not want to lose this opportunity, however, of saying a further word about studies.

I cannot emphasize too much the *importance of profound and continuous study* for the priesthood, and the development of study habits that will last through life. Our seminarians must be steeped in the Revelation of God. They must be philosophically and theologically literate. They must have not only an understanding of the faith, but they must be able to express and communicate that understanding.

American seminarians must be able to bring that understanding to bear on the forms of life and culture to be found in this land. We must have seminarians who develop a love of learning, a realization of the necessity of the life of the mind in the community born of the Revelation of God.

So now you know. The *centrality of the theology of the priesthood* is the key issue for seminaries. Whether members of the Visitation teams have been concerned with the spiritual formation of the seminarians, with their participation in the worship of God and their liturgical formation, with their study of philosophy or the various branches of theology, or with their apostolic and pastoral formation, the consensus of their opinion has converged on this point.

The announcement of the Apostolic Visitation, in fact, served as a stimulus. Its first fruit was to free the seminaries from an overload of "market forces" that wanted to use the seminaries to solve each and every need of catechetical and theological education in the Church today—and this in ignorance or in spite of the Vatican Council's affirmation of the necessity of specialized seminaries for priestly formation (*Optatam Totius*, n. 1). The announcement of the Visitation allowed the rectors and their colleagues to take control more fully of the central task entrusted to them.

The Contributors

Rev. Donald Senior, CP is president of Catholic Theological Union, Chicago, IL where he also serves as professor of New Testament. He received his doctorate from the University of Louvain in Belgium and has published numerous books and articles on biblical topics.

Sr. Agnes Cunningham, SSCM is professor of Patristic Theology and Early Christianity, at Mundelein Seminary, University of St. Mary of the Lake, Mundelein, IL. Former president of the Catholic Theological Society of America, she received her STD from the Catholic Faculty of Lyon, France and is the author of many books and articles on patristic studies.

Rev. John W. O'Malley, SJ is professor of Church History, Weston School of Theology, Cambridge, MA. He received his doctorate from Harvard University and has been the recipient of numerous awards and fellowships. A noted lecturer, he is the author of many books and articles on historical topics and is currently engaged in research on the history of religious orders and congregations.

Rev. Peter E. Fink, SJ is associate professor of Systematic Theology at Weston School of Theology, Cambridge, MA. He received his doctorate from Emory University, Atlanta, GA and is the author of numerous works in the area of sacramental theology.

Rev. Robert M. Schwartz is the spiritual director and dean of formation at the Saint Paul Seminary School of Divinity of the College of Saint Thomas, Saint Paul, MN. He received his STD in Spirituality from the Gregorian University, Rome. His current research focuses on the theology of priesthood as found in the documents of the Second Vatican Council.

Most Rev. J. Francis Stafford is the Archbishop of Denver, Co. Ordained a bishop in 1976, he has served as Auxiliary Bishop of Baltimore, MD and Bishop of Memphis, TN.

Most Rev. Daniel M. Buechlein, OSB has been Bishop of Memphis, TN since 1987. A monk of St. Meinrad's Abbey, he received the STL degree from the Benedictine University of Sant' Anselmo, Rome and served as president-rector of St. Meinrad's School of Theology, St. Meinrad, IN.

William Cardinal Baum is the Prefect of the Congregation for Seminaries and Catholic institutions in Vatican City. Cardinal Baum received his STD from the University of St. Thomas in Rome. Before assuming his Vatican post he served as Bishop of Springfield-Cape Girardeau, MO and as Archbishop of Washington, DC.